THE ANXIETY GUY'S GUIDE TO:

F*CK COPING
START HEALING

DENNIS SIMSEK

Note to the Reader: The content in this book is for informational purposes only and must not be regarded as medical advice. No action or inaction should be taken merely on the content of this information; instead, readers should consult appropriate health professionals on any matter relating to their health and well-being.

This book is dedicated to the survivors and warriors who deep down always believed that life could be more than just about suffering from anxiety.

TABLE OF CONTENTS

INTRODUCTION

"When you're looking for something wrong in everything, you're sure to find it."

I've died a million deaths in my mind, but never one in my physical reality. I've read a million minds, just to be wrong each time. I've catastrophized a million outcomes, just to be met with the opposite of my predictions. Welcome to my past life of anxiety. A place so dark that anyone within 5 feet of me would begin feeling a concerning emotional shift. A place of such repressed rage, horror, and bewilderment that even the slightest glance in the mirror would send me into an even deeper spiral toward helplessness. It was like living on an island by myself, but without the good weather, the coconuts, and the beach. Instead, I was stranded on this island with the blackest clouds hanging over me, the constant smell of durian gone bad (ugh), and a thousand island security guards who would never allow me to access even the thought of freedom.

I was diagnosed with an anxiety disorder in my mid-20s, and suffered greatly for 6 years after that diagnoses only to find healing within the span of 3 to 6 months in my early 30s. Although looking back on my life, the anxiety actually started when I was much younger, between the ages of 0-5, which is almost always the case with anxiety sufferers. In my first book, I went deep into my battle with anxiety.

"Me vs Myself" gave readers an in-depth and personal look into the rollercoaster ride that was my emotional distress. Many lessons have been learned since then, and I'll be presenting them to you here in F**k Coping, Start Healing.

Anxiety is a kind of like a splinter in your butt that stings all day, with only moments of relief. That's really the best way I can describe it. And if I were you, I would begin systematically slapping everyone in your life right now who comes to you thinking anxiety and stress are the same thing (just don't tell them I told you to do it; I'd like them to read this book, too). Anxiety, if you follow the steps in this book like your life depends on it (and most likely it does), will only be a temporary departure from your true identity. No, this long, dark tunnel that you're in right now doesn't have to be traveled indefinitely. There are ways out — even if other people have told you that you can only manage and cope with your anxiety. Those people have either gotten their expectations rejected one too many times, or are too lazy to look deeper within. Oh, and if you haven't noticed already, I'm not going to hold anything back in this book. Because there's already enough shit floating around in the anxiety recovery and self-help world. I value your time, and I value my time. And I will give you everything I have as long as you promise that you'll do the same, even if your mind wanders off to the land of self-doubt from time to time (and believe me, it will).

Together, you and I are headed toward an inner transformation. It begins with an inner awakening followed by a rebirth, and then by moving through life with a brand-new pair of lenses. This is a process that holds no timeline for your healing. It's a journey where the balance between your desire for certainty and faith in uncertainty meet. I like to call this a flow state. It's the place where fighting with your current thinking patterns, your rocky past, your physical sensations, and your emotions become a thing of the past. You will find harmony between your conscious mind, your subconscious mind, and your body, and the results will be nothing short of miraculous. Right now, you're likely in a place of great desperation and dissatisfaction. You might even be at rock bottom, seeing that your life is passing you by quickly as morning turns to night with very little fulfillment in between. This is actually a great place to start because there's nowhere to go but up. Together we will forgive those who need to be forgiven (especially you), release the guilt that needs to be released, and set you on the path toward healing. I'm excited for you because I'm presenting to you what has worked for the thousands of anxiety sufferers who I've had the privilege of helping through their journey to healing. Give yourself full permission to go slowly and gently through this book with an open and loving mind.

Now it's time for you to f**k coping and start healing!

Dennis

CHAPTER 1:

Introduction to Rapid Intuitive Conditioning (RIC)

"The moment of greatest progress for someone with anxiety is when they abandon the formula that's not working for them that they've been hoping will work for them someday."

It's essential that we start with a clear understanding of what Rapid Intuitive Conditioning (RIC) is because this book is highly focused around this strategy. RIC is derived from many of the best teachings within ancient wisdom and present methodologies. It's the sum of all that works — and works the fastest — all rolled up into this powerful book.

I don't know about you, but during my years with an anxiety disorder, there was one thing that frustrated me more than anything else: When I asked for help from a coach or therapist, they sounded like programmed robots with readily prepared answers rather than truly focusing on my targeted needs. I remember asking a couple of other clients who were seeing the same CBT therapist as I was (don't get me wrong, I love CBT, and CBT has a place in healing) what strategy they had received, and it was the same as mine! I was shocked. I lost all hope right then and there. Was this a common practice, or just one therapist's approach? Was this as good as it was going to get? The answers would show up in time.

I developed RIC to be a process where every anxiety sufferer would be listened to, understood, and responded to depending on his or her PERSONAL needs. I remember how it felt, not to be able to build trust in my mentors because they couldn't relate to my disorder — most of them had never experienced the kind of anxiety that I had suffered with. So, no more frustration, a brand-new approach is born through RIC, and the foundation of it all is responsive coaching rather than preprogrammed coping methods.

RIC targets harmony between the conscious, more intellectual mind, and the subconscious, more emotional mind. It will show you that you have options in your ways of thinking and perceiving; it puts power back into your conscious, more rational mind so you can see through your current conditioning.

RIC recognizes that each person's character/identity is built around what he or she does most often, and what is of the highest importance to him or her. Through this understanding of how character is built, we come to see that a person's struggle with anxiety isn't cemented for life; rather it is caused by a lack of the proper clarity/understanding and the tools needed to recondition a new identity.

Now let's break down what Rapid Intuitive Conditioning means:

Rapid – Helping you understand that change can happen faster than you might currently believe. We do this by shifting your core beliefs at the deepest level, therefore making a "nice idea" become part of your overall belief system.

Intuitive – Trusting in your own intuition to bring out the right formula for healing depending on your targeted needs. The goal is to help you become your own coach and mentor so you can recognize and respond to daily challenges. This intuitive side tends to get lost along the way when we're looking for outside guidance rather than looking and listening within to understand ourselves and our situation better.

Conditioning – Building relentless conditioning toward total change in your core beliefs and identity. As the conditioning process picks up more steam and repetition along the way, you'll begin to see that you're not actually broken, and you never were, just a little bent. You will understand that what's bent can be unbent, and you will feel a sense of humbleness because of what you have gone through, and empowerment in who you're becoming.

In this book, you will learn how to be your own RIC coach for anxiety (and any other inner challenges you face). It's important for you to be able to guide yourself because otherwise, you'll constantly be looking for a magic wand from someone or something else. We don't want that. Instead, I want you to take the words "don't believe everything you think and feel" to a deep level.

Here are some of the main principles within the teachings of RIC:

We have two thought systems, not just one: analytical and survival

The Greek philosopher Heraclitus reminds us that, "To be even-minded is the greatest virtue." As much as your survival system may be working overtime at the moment, know that through this book, we will be working toward balancing out these two systems. When this balance shows up, so does harmony between the emotions and logic. At that point, you will be no longer led by either, but intuitively sense what to do at the time. This is the spine of the RIC teaching framework.

See each challenge from a frequency, vibrational, and energetic perspective

There are only two things you can do: give or receive energy. The question is, what energy are you giving and receiving? RIC teaches you that your outer experiences have everything to do with your inner experiences. As we begin shifting the vibrational frequency that you are emitting into the world, your outside circumstances and perceptions start to change. All of a sudden, the world will look different, and you will sense a feeling of being limitless rather than being tied down by limitations.

To come to a new definition of the word trauma

When I use the word "trauma" in this book, I'm not just referring to war veterans suffering from PTSD. Trauma includes any event that you perceived as unsafe; when you felt helpless. It can range from something simple, like having your toy taken away when you were a child, to

7

more complex situations like being neglected by a distracted caregiver. Trauma can be anything when we see the experience not from our adult perspective but from the child's perspective all over again. This child still lives within each of us and needs the proper reflection and guidance to match the current age of a person.

One of America's greatest healers of back pain was Dr. John Sarno. He uncovered how trauma and repressed emotion (leading to stress and anxiety) could develop into chronic back pain in the body. Science is just now starting to catch up with Dr. Sarno's work, but it certainly won't be easy to convince today's professionals of the possibility of psychosomatic effects, rather than structural issues, when it comes to pain and discomfort. The good news is that trauma doesn't have to be permanent when we understand how to communicate with this wounded inner child. In later chapters, we will look at reframing, a process that holds the key to renegotiating trauma and taking back your power for good.

The stronger the emotion, the stronger the storage will be within the subconscious mind

The higher the intensity of a person's emotions (whether positive or negative), the deeper the feeling and memory get stored within the infinite storage system in the mind and the body. Our emotions are the signals that get sent out into the world and bring us more of what we're feeling. For example, the universe takes our emotions very literally, so we must begin learning how to take back control of our emotional state moment by moment.

The subconscious mind will create blind spots to prevent you from seeing and understanding opposing information that goes against your core beliefs

In a nutshell, your negative beliefs can make you blind to what else is possible. But I'm sure you already know this if you suffer from anxiety. For example, take the story by one of my favorite monks, Ajahn Brahm, who tells the tale of the two bad bricks:

Once upon a time, there was a child who set out to build a treehouse with bricks. He gathered all his bricks, set a schedule for himself each day to build his treehouse so that he could play in it with all his friends. As he finished the treehouse, he was extremely excited and tremendously proud of himself; he couldn't wait to share his treehouse with others. As he was taking a tour around his newly built treehouse, he noticed that there were two bricks missing right in the center of the treehouse. Everything else looked perfect except for what he referred to as the "two bad bricks." He was distraught, annoyed, and angered with himself. He couldn't believe he made such a big mistake, and he felt like he ruined the entire treehouse. As a few friends came around to see his treehouse, they loved it, they danced around it and played in it, but the child who had built the treehouse wasn't as excited anymore. He shouted, "Don't you see the two bad bricks! This treehouse is awful; it's incomplete and broken." The other kids had never even noticed the two bad bricks, and upon seeing them, they replied with, "They're just two missing bricks, that's all. The treehouse still works, it's safe and fun." The child began getting this sort of response as more and more kids started showing up, and he began turning his focus toward the hundreds of other good bricks rather than just the two bad bricks. As he did this, his perceptions over the treehouse shifted, and he began feeling proud of himself again and learned a few valuable lessons. Those lessons were that mistakes are OK, and what you focus on will determine how you feel.

How someone views the world is their personal reality

Everyone has a unique way of seeing the world, and it must be respected and understood for a positive change to show up. If you currently live with beliefs that disempower you, your internal and external reality will fit with these beliefs. Your identity/personality is a result of what you believe to be the truth, as well as the positive, neutral, or negative associations you've made between things. In essence, your viewpoints over who you are, what people mean, and what life is all about colors the path that you're on. If you look at your inner and outer results and find that you are unsatisfied with what you sense, it's time to change the components that make up your identity.

People interpret sensory data based on how they feel and how they perceive their memories

Anxiety is due to interpretation — not the way you feel, or what happens on the outside. Opinions, reactions, and comments have more to do with someone's past, rather than what's currently taking place. A person with built-up negative momentum from the day will interpret sensory information differently from someone with positive momentum. Also, the way a person perceives their past has a lot to do with how they perceive the present. These are recognitions that usually fall out of conscious awareness, but must be respected.

Flexibility in thinking is the gateway to freedom

The faster you can open up your mind and heart to other possibilities, the quicker you will heal. Healing anxiety requires an open mind; there's no way around it. Either you begin doing things that help you to perceive your past, present, and future differently, or you're stuck with a narrow-minded view of yourself and the world. In my healing journey over anxiety, I noticed something interesting: my first two or three interpretations of something were the furthest thing from the truth. The more patient I was, as I paused and waited for more options to show up in my mind, the more balanced my interpretations became. It wasn't until the fourth or fifth thought that I found the truth of the situation; the first few thoughts were that of a survival response, not a rational one.

The opposite of fear is love

Marianne Williamson once said, "Love is to humans what water is to plants." Love is almost always the missing ingredient in the emotional state known as anxiety. A lack of love by the people who we needed it the most from when we were young, is by far the most common reason people look for fulfillment in a relationship. Are they truly in love with the other person? Or are they the ones to fill the need leftover from childhood? This kind of honesty sometimes hurts but is an essential part of the healing process. On this journey, you will have many opportunities to pick either fear of love, and if you pick fear, it might fall in line with what's most common in your life. However, if you choose love, it will be uncomfortable, and you will get a sense of moving toward an unfamiliar place in your life. That is the exact place you need to be for long-term, positive change.

I urge you to study and understand these RIC principles as you shift your mindset. RIC is an integration of powerful attitudes and responses that can create flexibility in your way of thinking and acting that leads to major internal shifts. During my journey through anxiety, I realized that with every new epiphany came another introduction back into parts of myself that had been lost. At one point, in those dark years, I felt I was losing touch with who I was, and it led me to question God and the reason for life. The more I questioned, the more confused I got. Once I started integrating RIC into my life, I found what I was actually looking for: peace. Up until that time, chaos ruled my life. Whether it was chaos inside of me, or drama in someone else's life, it didn't matter; I was always in the presence of chaos. During my anxiety years, I became overly interested in news topics like where the latest protests and terrorist attacks were happening, and what my favorite celebrities were doing. I rationalized why I did it too. I told myself that knowing where protests were happening helped me understand government corruption better, that keeping up with terrorism protected me from visiting those cities, and that watching celebs gave me a sense of not being so crazy since they were all anxious too. We can justify just about anything. We grab ideas from thin air and begin believing they are the truth.

The biggest problem I was experiencing was that I was way too comfortable in my discomfort.

Did I need all that drama? I thought I did; it fulfilled what I felt I needed. But did it really? Or did I just have too much time on my hands? When we don't direct our minds toward a clear and concise direction, the mind will revert to searching for the next thing that must be feared; this is how anxiety works.

People often confuse the act of distraction with purpose, thinking that when they distract themselves, they are living in harmony with their purpose when, in fact, it's just a temporary coverup. With distraction, symptoms may lessen and disappear temporarily, but the subconscious mind is still holding on to experiences from your past that you haven't yet reframed and renegotiated. This doesn't mean you have to process your past in a way that potentially re-traumatizes you. By utilizing the reframing methods of RIC, you can gently and compassionately begin taking note of the things you are denying and avoiding in your life.

I want you to know two very important things: I believe in you, and I'm on your side. Through this book, I will show you the way toward healing anxiety. As you embrace the fundamentals of RIC, you will bring forth what you've been hiding for too long. Allow this truth to replace your fear-based conditioning as life opens its arms to you in full embrace. Do not fear love anymore, please, but instead allow it in. To express what you hold within is to travel leaps and bounds through anxiety.

In the course of healing, it's necessary to talk about our past traumas, but only a little. It's also necessary to talk about our present emotional distress, but, again, only a little. If you feel comfortable sharing these things with awakened people, they get a glimpse into your inner environment, and the people who've succeeded as you wish to succeed can provide what's needed — love and acceptance. If you talk too much, you only dig yourself into a deeper hole. A balance between talk and action is needed. This is why 95% of today's anxiety forums and self-help groups prove to be more harmful than helpful; they focus too much on coping and talking about distress rather than on healing. I know it's tempting to get a seemingly quick fix of anxiety relief from an online forum, but escape these environments at once; don't even think twice about it. You may feel an initial sense of loss, but in the long run, you will face yourself the way you need to in order to heal.

RIC is as much a spiritual path as it is a mental, emotional, and physical one. Without the companionship of a spiritual guide, you are at a tremendous disadvantage in healing anxiety. This is because a big part of the change process depends on your ability to let in what you've been told you can't tap into or doesn't exist. This level of uncertainty has been avoided and banished for far too long, and you've paid the price by feeling you need to create change all by yourself. The spiritual path leads to enlightenment, which is closer than most people think it is. Enlightenment is a place of pure bliss, without the need for anything to occur from the outside. This is a mental space that has the potential even to look death in the face and smile back. This becomes the moment of greatest freedom.

Enlightenment through RIC comes from an ongoing practice of asking the question "what is this trying to teach me?" From this point of reference, you will come to a deeper understanding that there's no such thing as a bad experience; there's only life. Everything, no matter whether you deem it good or bad, will be experienced, and the only question is how you process that experience. Processing all difficult experiences from the angle of life, rather than loss, will set you free. That's because inner freedom is learned; most of us are not born into it. We develop the skills that lead us to inner freedom when we process experiences from the viewpoint of it being life, nothing more, nothing less.

But true inner peace seems out of reach for a lot of people today because guilt has become far too common a response. Guilt? For what? How dare you blame yourself for what took place in your childhood. You had no conscious faculty to be able to deal with those experiences at the time, but now, that inner, wounded child lives within you, and he or she is begging for a new direction.

Another common practice is feeling guilty for saying the "wrong" thing during a conversation. What implies that something is wrong anyway? The fact that it doesn't fall in line with the expectations of the other person you're dialoguing with? You tiptoe through life looking to stay in line for as long as possible as your anxiety builds only to become more confused as to why you feel more and more anxious. If you keep this up, you will be lying on your deathbed years from now, and it will hit you like a ton of bricks that the world can't be pleased, and it was all just an illusion. But by that time, you'll already be onto your next level of consciousness and wish you could have taken the teachings of RIC to heart and began questioning everything.

Life is what you believe it is. You are what you believe you are. And the result of this moment depends on your interpretation of it. I want to put you back into the driver's seat of your life; to access the inner resources you need; to access control of what can be controlled, and to place faith over what you can't.

Summary:

- RIC is a flexible approach to healing that respects the personal journey of each anxiety sufferer and directs him or her according to their particular needs. It doesn't have pre-determined responses and tools; it's flexible.
- RIC asks important questions to spur on conscious thinking, which then takes the sufferer toward a deeper understanding of the formula they use to create their inner experiences.
- RIC is centered around communicating directly with the younger version of the anxiety sufferer to provide safety for them over what took place in the past, what's taking place in the moment, and how to look toward the future.
- Within the RIC teachings, the mental, emotional, physical, and spiritual bodies are all taken into account toward a strategic plan for change. When all four categories are working in sync within a person, a new identity has been designed, and the actions that follow become more and more naturally positive.
- In RIC, setbacks are seen as inevitable, and mental, behavioral, and imaginative preparation take priority over "winging it."

CHAPTER 2:

Anxiety Uncovered

*"Healing anxiety always was and
always will be an inside job."*

Welcome to anxiety, the greatest distraction from living a pleasant life. When it comes to anxiety, most people think it's something they just have to cope with, perhaps for the rest of their lives. There are many reasons why. The first lines of anxiety treatment are failing miserably; support groups online and offline do nothing more than focus on symptoms; family and friends don't understand how to help due to their inexperience with anxiety; kids are being subliminally and unconsciously programmed with irrational fear; and more and more coping inventions are coming out by the day. No wonder so many people are left wondering where they can run to for safety, and what they can do to make themselves feel better immediately.

Don't buy into the idea that managing anxiety is the best that you can do. F**k that!

Yes, we live in a confusing and stressful world right now, and there are people out there (with the best of intentions) who think they are gurus because they've reversed their stress a few times. It's hard to know who to trust and where to turn. This can lead to information overload. When that happens, the survival and emotional parts of the brain redirect their focus toward any immediate threat in the environment. And here's where anxiety proves itself to be a liar. It's a liar because it's only trying to keep you safe; move your genes forward. It's looking after your survival, trying to protect you. Even though it might not feel like it right now, this system loves you and wants to keep you happy, but never at the expense of your safety.

I know from experience that anxiety sucks; it was pure hell, but I healed from it, and so can you. I understand how hard it can be when you have stuff to do, and people are relying on you. How difficult it is to do anything properly, and with full absorption, while at the same time battling this inner demon that relentlessly shows up every waking minute of every day. You've tried logic, convincing yourself that you're safe. You've tried talking to someone about it, and still, you may be left asking yourself, "What am I doing wrong?"

During my 6-year journey through a multitude of anxiety disorders, I found it difficult just getting through each day. I had a hard time focusing on tasks, it was tough to recognize how my bodily sensations and my negative emotional states were overtaking my thinking patterns, and I beat myself up over and over again for replaying the same demoralizing self-defeating habits. The victim mindset was strong; feelings of helplessness grew by the minute. Drudgingly taking my shower, I would wonder what would happen if I fell? Would anyone save me? Speeding through my so-called "breakfast," and then getting into my car, I focused on how I would get through the maze of anxiety that day. I began to recognize that I could experience small spurts of inner freedom the more I engulfed myself in my work, but it took me farther away from calmness. The formula was: Faster = productive, surviving the day = the goal, pleasing others = connection, and a sense of belonging. Anxiety makes everything 10 times worse. Wait, no, 100 times worse. A simple walk outside turns into the fear of potentially getting hit by a car, or having a heart attack, or the dreaded and uncomfortable run-in with someone you know.

"Why does everyone around me look so … normal?" I would ask myself.

Looking at all of these so-called normal people, I'd feel anger and jealousy toward them. I built up a case in my head about how bad I had it. In my mind, the world was out to get me. There was no hope, and no matter what I tried, I would fall short, so why bother. Can you relate?

Let's get one thing out of the way right now: Anxiety isn't stress. Most anxiety sufferers don't fully understand or accept that fact, and they often downplay the severity of their pain. Using the word "stress" to relate some of their suffering to others sounds a lot more socially acceptable. There's a lot of reluctance in sharing what's really taking place inside, that is, if we have the courage to tell anyone at all. Unfortunately, the general response is "you worry too much," or "just don't think about it," along with the suggestion to use "positive thinking." First off, positive thinking doesn't work, and if you could stop thinking about it, don't you think you would have by now? Anxiety is a much more stubborn beast than others realize. Positive thinking, in the general sense, doesn't work because it's fake. I don't care how many times you look in the mirror and repeat the words "I'm beautiful." At a core belief and identity level, if you think you're ugly, you're ugly. The same goes for anxiety. If you repeat words like "I am safe" when, in fact, nothing in your present or past proves the safety you're trying to project, it gets rejected by your mind.

Do you know how to find out what you truly think of yourself? During the first 15 minutes after you wake up each day, look in the mirror and stare into your own eyes. Then listen. This is a very powerful exercise. What thoughts show up automatically? That's you, and that's what's holding you back.

Fake it till you make it doesn't work for the vast majority of anxiety sufferers since you can't fake your way into convincing your subconscious mind. These deeply held beliefs about yourself and the world are the laws you unconsciously follow daily; it's like starting a new sport and wanting to change the rules of the game. You can't. Those are the rules, and they are set in stone (for now); if you want to play that sport, you have to abide by them. This is the way the deepest parts of you see your reality. That doesn't mean all hope is lost though, anxiety will go away once you have the understanding and application of what's taught in this book. But my one question to you is, have you hit rock bottom yet?

Desperation and dissatisfaction are the starting points to change.

When you are ready to do WHATEVER it takes to change, only then will you change. Basking in your discomfort and fear can become so habitual that some people never get to what I call "the point of no return." This is where you end the franticness and look deeper within. Because without this emotional signal to your nervous system, the message that change is necessary doesn't get sent. You can't just think your way out of severe anxiety, because at the level of severe anxiety, you're too invested in your supercharged nervous emotions to gather any kind of momentum through thought alone.

Desperation looks extreme fear in the face and says "bring it on, I'm done running." A person then survives the experience of looking fear in the face and lives on. This adds one tick out of potentially a hundred more that is needed to convince the subconscious mind that change is safe. Let's be honest, it took tremendous unconscious commitment to get to this level of severe anxiety, and it will take the same conscious commitment (as well as an understanding of how to communicate with the deepest parts of yourself) to go an opposing route. This should excite you, which it probably just did, followed by all the reasons you shouldn't get too excited about change. That is a conscious response followed by the subconscious reaction, and it's time to get them harmonized correctly.

These 3 main types of anxiety disorders are usually interconnected during the struggle:

Panic disorder – Defined by severe states of panic, leading to negative states in the body, and then an overwhelming feeling of needing to run away or escape. Panic disorder is like tiptoeing through the day, hoping the worst (a heart attack, heightened sensations, recognition by others, etc.) doesn't show up.

Social anxiety disorder – Here it becomes hard to function and cope in social settings. This is usually caused by insecurities and a lack of confidence leading to the fear of judgment by others. Social anxiety sufferers think they can read minds, but they're not good at it. People may be complimenting them on the outside, but to the social anxiety sufferer, those same people are ridiculing them on the inside. These negative beliefs create a vicious cycle that can lead to the sufferer staying within their safe zone, so they don't have to feel that others are judging them.

Generalized anxiety disorder (GAD) – GAD doesn't particularly lead people to avoid certain situations, unlike other forms of anxiety. It can affect many different areas of a person's life and is more of a general sense of anxiety about one or more aspects of a person's life. Constant internal chatter in the mind can accompany GAD.

I had all three of the above, as well as other "disorders" that we'll touch on in this book. A common misconception about these types of vulnerabilities is that they are signs of weakness. In reality, vulnerability is the key to growth because we must learn how to accept and be vulnerable on this journey. It's a sign of strength and courage. Anxiety is like feeling you're naked everywhere you go. You've lost control, and can't gain it back, so you start trying to control more and more things in the hope of feeling some sanity and less of the feeling that you're going to "lose it."

As you'll recognize going through this book, anxiety is very much not your fault, but it's your responsibility to overcome. The amazing thing is that every belief you know about (conscious) or don't know about (subconscious) has a feeling attached to it. That feeling is connected to a frequency and energy in your body. As the feelings in your body change, the frequencies in your body change. This is the "rapid" part of RIC. Change can happen rapidly once you integrate a well-rounded system into your life. As you go deeper into this book, you'll recognize more and more that your brain and body are one entity — they are not separate. It's a feedback loop, and with anxiety, the brain speaks to the body, and the body speaks to the brain, creating the emotional arousal that begins pulling your focus toward everything in the world that maintains your anxious state.

When it comes to anxiety, one of the main pitfalls is that we have thoughts about thoughts and feelings about feelings. What, exactly, does that mean? Most of the time, it's not the initial thought or feeling that creates anxiety. It's the add-ons on top of what came initially that cause more evidence to accumulate around the perception of danger. We feel threatened when there's no real threat around. Our minds and bodies work as one unit to deter us from enjoying the moment and instead make us believe that:

- We can read minds and therefore know exactly what another person is thinking about us.
- Our thoughts are exactly connected to how the outcome will turn out.
- There's only one potential outcome for every given situation.

Anxiety sufferers find themselves justifying their irrational fears to themselves and others to explain their behavior. For example, I literally convinced my fiancée that I had a physical illness and that our relationship would only last a few years before I died. This is the power of holding onto the thoughts and images we play out; it can make us believe anything. I was always slumped over, always breathing shallow, always pessimistic, and full of inner rage from my past. In order to explain this behavior to myself and others, I had to have a story to back it up. We all become the stories we tell ourselves. If you want to change your life, start telling yourself a different story, take a step back, and wait. You will begin to justify the truth behind your new story as your perceptions and physical health begin to respond positively. Anxiety isn't a life sentence; it's a bundle of habits that you're too scared to alter because of conscious and subconscious beliefs.

Below are some of the beliefs I held that I was consciously aware of:

- I've suffered too long.
- I'm getting too old to change.
- My dad had anxiety, so I must learn to live with this.
- I don't deserve to feel good because I didn't earn it.
- I feel that others may want me to stay this way forever; if I change, they might not want to be friends with me anymore.
- Anxiety is my protective mechanism; it keeps me safe from uncertain events.
- It's a part of who I am.
- Life is more certain with fear.

This type of list doesn't have an end for many anxiety sufferers. These are beliefs that a person may or may not be aware of. You can't change something that you're unaware of, so you must bring these beliefs into your awareness and begin questioning their legitimacy. You'll find that they're not legit, they're just ideas. But just because you know they're ideas doesn't mean your anxiety will go away just like that. Remember, it's a convincing game, and the subconscious mind (the boss) is the one to convince. Here's an example:

A high school football player is about to play in a football game (in this case, the player is the anxiety sufferer). During the game, a college scout shows up out of the blue to watch the player to potentially recruit him to his respective college (the subconscious mind). If the player doesn't turn in a performance that signifies his ability to compete in college, he won't get recruited. Likewise, if the anxiety sufferer doesn't convince the subconscious mind that a new identity is safe to take on, the deeper mind won't change its ways. The football scout will want to make sure that the player is the right fit, so he'll stop by a number of times, just like the subconscious mind will be taking notes on the commitment level and potential safety over an anxiety sufferer's new way of thinking, speaking, acting, and imagining.

RIC recognizes that the health of our nervous system is dictated by the feelings that we experience the most often. If you keep feeling bad, you are projecting the need for more bad. If you keep feeling good, you are projecting the need for more good. What you feel dictates who you are, so we must begin learning how to go from bad, to neutral, to good within the framework of RIC. To begin doing this, we must understand that the mind and you are not the same. You are not your mind; you are separate from your mind. It's important to understand this and step back to observe your thinking from the side of your higher self.

Your higher self is less judgmental and more observant; it takes in all the possibilities and sees positive potentials. Your higher self is the real you since you will fight many battles in your life that never pose any real danger. Your higher self understands this, but your artificial, fear-based self doesn't yet. The limiting beliefs you have only hold power because you say yes to them and agree with them. The moment you disagree and replace those limiting beliefs in connection with beginning to respect yourself at a deeper level, your limits cease to exist. No one, not even your own mind, can make you feel inferior without your permission. Always remember that.

Summary:

- Don't believe everything you think or feel.
- Anxiety is built consciously and unconsciously, and what's built can always be taken down, creating space to build something new in its place.
- Desperation is the starting point to healing anxiety and becoming the greatest version of you.
- Self-defeatism has no place in the life of someone healing from anxiety.
- Positive thinking is a default response to anxiety but rarely leads to long-term positive changes. The positive thought becomes too general and not specific to the situation; the emotions rarely accompany the positive thought, and a person

rarely acts in line with that thought leading to reverting to catastrophic future thinking again.

CHAPTER 3:

The 'I Am' Model

"Anxiety makes people strangers to themselves."

Imagine how sad it would be to walk around for the rest of your life as an artificial version of who you really are. Well, that's what anxiety brings to the table. We dupe ourselves into thinking, speaking, acting, and imagining what we believe will please others the most. Many anxiety sufferers are no different from a programmed robot. They wake up each day thinking the same things and believing the same truths about who they are and what they're capable of. Little do they realize that while in the anxiety trance, their limiting self-concept is a result of a formula — one they've unconsciously (for the most part) invested in over a long time. When they come to an understanding that anxiety isn't who they are, but instead related to things they're doing that's causing this torturous emotional state, they're in shock! One of my past clients said, "You mean, I've been living a lie?" I replied, "Yes, and the only reason why you haven't seen it until now is because no one told you the difference."

As strange as it sounds, at one point, I was getting comfortable in my anxious skin. My anxiety persona seemed to be paying off in various ways. It was the reason why I only worked 25 hours a week rather than 40. I could play the anxiety card when people wanted me to do things I didn't want to do. I had a reason for not pursuing my goals. I could spend hours watching Netflix. I even got others to do my laundry for me. I had fallen in love with all the sympathy I was getting, which replaced my unmet needs from childhood (mainly from dad). This is what's referred to as secondary gains. These are the reasons we do what we do — it provides us with the opportunity to fill needs that might not get met any other way. Take a moment to let that one sink in, because it's heavy. Oh, and you can stop denying that this is true; every anxiety sufferer does it in varying degrees. This is because we fulfill our unmet needs from childhood either in negative or in positive ways. In negative ways, some people may unconsciously and consciously create disease in their body so that their mom can finally show them a little love. Positively we can meet those same unmet needs through healthy contributions toward other people's lives, like giving a speech.

I think you're beginning to see how easy it can be to get stuck between the conscious mind wanting change (for the most part), and the unconscious mind reminding us of all we're going to have to give up: good and bad. It's like the old Archie comics where Archie is torn between being in a relationship with either Betty or Veronica (yes, I'm an '80s child). Betty takes every opportunity to show Archie her affection, and the beautiful life they could have together (this is freedom from anxiety). Veronica, on the other hand, plays Archie like a puppet, flaunts her sexiness more, and has sucked Archie into doing all she demands of him. Why doesn't Archie just go for Betty, and live happily ever after? Because Archie is addicted to suffering, that's why. He believes that happiness must be slaved for and earned. So every time Veronica comes around, his core beliefs match up with the way she treats him — kind of like you and anxiety. Freedom could be an easier path than you think, but your belief system makes you think it can't be, and that suffering has been far too consistent of an occurrence. But it's not all your fault. Your system will create blind spots to whatever came first at childhood, anything that goes against what you believe to be true, and what you've acted on the most. If you're an anxiety sufferer, walk down the street and I promise you that your focus will turn to the sign on the building that reads "Have you gotten your blood tests done lately? You never know these days." Or you'll sort for and become laser-focused on the kid who's playing in a tree that looks like he may fall (even though he won't, and the kid's got better balance than you). The emotional states that we walk around with daily will determine what we consciously pay attention to, and what we don't. This is called your emotional refractory period, and it's working all the time.

The emotional refractory period is a filter designed to re-trigger the emotional state you're already in, and it's relentless at doing this. Next time you get into an argument with your wife, husband, or friend, notice how, after the disagreement, everything they say to you (even nice things) still piss you off! The nervous system seeks to maintain equilibrium. Whatever state it's in, it wants to hold onto, so it will change the priority of information in the environment and alter the words you hear from others. Your perceptual filters change, and the way you take in and make sense of information in the social world gets completely altered.

This perfectly translates into the cycle of anxiety and the RIC-based "I am" model. So, you can stop blaming yourself for the constant sensitivity you feel and start blaming a mechanism within you that's doing what it's supposed to. I can hear you now, "Damn you, emotional refractory period!" But remember, it also works for the opposing emotions as well. When you have a tremendous moment of gratitude or a rush of pleasure, everything you see, hear, feel, smell, and taste is wonderful. Think about your latest orgasm if you want further proof.

To get someone to a place where they have firmed up their "I am's" takes a lot of practice. In the beginning, it was just a hiccup, a moment, a challenge. Over time, as those moments became more common, it turned into your personality. The "I am" model identifies five stages through a person's life that brings them to the point of believing that they are, in this case, anxiety.

1) The Addiction To Suffering

Ask yourself, "do I have an underlying addiction to suffering? And do I constantly sabotage all the good that comes my way (internally within feelings, or externally for experiences)?" The addiction to suffering is common, don't worry, you're not the only one (by a long shot). Much of it is due to the people throughout your life who have conditioned you into believing that:

- Without struggle, you'll never amount to anything.
- Without some type of pain (mental, emotional, even physical), you're not sacrificing enough for the greater good.
- There's no such thing as a straight path toward anything. Everything you'll ever want takes hard work (this was a tough one for me to reframe).

In addition, there's the power of habit. Whatever's been most consistently applied and practiced in your life becomes the template that gets matched up with every other future similar situation. Your system detects a situation, goes into its filing cabinet, retrieves information based on what was there first and practiced the most, and does everything in its power to make the person do the same thing. This strengthens a person's core beliefs (subconscious) each time the person acts on their feelings and thoughts. The stronger a person's core beliefs, the more difficult it becomes for the person's conscious, rational, and logical side to intervene and change it. This is one of the biggest reasons why positive thinking alone doesn't work. There's not enough juice, strength, and emotion behind the thought to effectively bring it from a head level (to think) to a heart level (to feel and believe).

More and more people are becoming addicted to chaos, drama, and fear. At every moment, we are bombarded with information that forces us to believe that we're never safe, and we must tiptoe our way through life — what a crock. We weren't born this way; we learned to be this way. And through our unique electromagnetic energy, which can be measured by today's superconducting quantum interference devices (SQUIDS), we're giving off information constantly that can be detected within 6 feet of a person's human body (heartmath.org provides the studies for this). We're affecting everyone around us (and the same for them to you). That wounded inner child never stood a chance. It was inevitable not only at the moment you came to this world but even before that, that your emotions would lead to the addiction to suffering. While you were in the womb, in fact, the emotions that mommy felt, you also felt, the energetic communication between your authority figures you picked up on, and you came to this word feeling like a mistake without uttering your first word.

How do I know this? Because I've worked with thousands of people worldwide who reveal it to me when I put them into an altered state of consciousness. During the hypnotic process (as the conscious mind is still very much attuned), I regress them to the beginning, the initial sensitizing event (ISE) that has everything to do with their addiction to suffering today. Consistently, they're back in mommy's tummy. Those 9 months already began fine-tuning their identities. That initial sensitizing event would lead to subsequent events that were very similar to the original first pie-in-the face, and no, they weren't "accidents." This is known as the "moment of separation" in the Course In Miracles and can only rarely be recalled through conscious intervention.

It was one big snowball effect after that, as we'll tap into more as we progress through this book. Once those original subconscious programs are set in place, they will look to be fulfilled at every opportunity. This is referred to as "the calling" by Stephen Parkhill, author of the book "Answer Cancer." Even if an idea or action may be better for you in the short term or long term, if it doesn't align with the subconscious programs, they get rejected. Therefore, you see people going through multiple anxiety disorders throughout their lives. When one irrational fear and potential threat has lost its ability to control the person's actions, the next one is right around the corner. And the amazing thing is that your subconscious mind-body loves you unconditionally! It just can't differentiate between what may be good for you and what's bad for you. All it can go by is what was encoded into your nervous system between conception and the age of 7 (many say 5, but we'll be flexible).

2) Worry

The "I am" model leads us to the second stage, which is worry. As the addiction to suffering gets installed into a person, it leads to the need to "stand guard" no matter what. The most routine future experiences, such as taking your spouse on a date, going to see a movie, or having tea at a café, turns into a life or death future scenario. Here's how my anxious mind worked when I was about to head to the local café, during my years of sensitivity and anxiety:

- I wondered how many people would be there. If it was over 10, it was "too much" for me to handle.
- Would the barista want to spark a spontaneous conversation with me? If that were the case, what would I say back?
- Would the tea be too hot? Forcing me to stay stuck with people I didn't know for longer, oh the pain!

- What if I ran into someone from my old high school days? What if they detected my anxiousness and began spreading the word that Dennis was crazy!
- If I spilled any of my tea, I would embarrass myself to the point of never being able to go back. I'll be the laughingstock of the city!

Quite the imagination, I know. Worry kept me busy and ate up most of my day. I can't even imagine the amount of fun, peace, and even sex I could have had with all that time worrying over such silly possibilities. But that's what anxiety sufferers do! They apply laser-like focus to the potential catastrophe of an experience that they're in or going into, if the experience is one that isn't too common in their recent lives.

Let's dive even deeper into this worrying habit. I like to use the term "depleted but wired" to describe what life with chronic anxiety is really like — depleted because most anxiety sufferers rely solely on willpower, grit, and force to deal with their issues. Roy Baumeister, the author of the book "Willpower," reminds us that we have a finite amount of willpower, so it's no wonder these sufferers come home at the end of the day ready for a pizza and beer to give them something to feel good about. This kind of depletion isn't just physical, though; it's emotional because, at the more extreme levels of anxiety, people stop feeling altogether. And mental because they no longer have the ability to make sense of the answers they need to hear that are right in front of them. The power is literally sucked out of them completely. They are locked into a vibration that makes the climb toward freedom steeper and steeper. This vibration also gets picked up by others. No wonder it's so easy to boss you around as you feel the deepest levels of inferiority imaginable. But don't fret; this too shall pass, as I know how ready you are for change.

Then there's the wired part: The anxiety sufferer gets the sense that the moment they give up their guard, danger will strike. You see this with hypochondriacs (health anxiety) who are constantly misinterpreting their physical sensations of anxiety, thinking that a physical ailment is imminent. You'll also see this at play during conversations. Every word the anxiety sufferer utters is analyzed to death prior to, during, and after the conversation (which is tiring, to say the least). If someone else criticizes them, they'll internalize it and fall even deeper into the black hole of doom. So, confrontation of any kind must be avoided at all costs because the interpretation is that it would be too challenging to be able to deal with. As well, trust in their problem-solving abilities is at an all-time low.

Reality becomes so very distorted, generalized, and deleted. Distorted in order to fall back in line with the common theme of over-worrying ("it's not that way, it's this way"). Generalized in order to group things together to make unconscious labeling easier in the future (good, bad, ugly, pretty, etc.). Deleted to conform to the dire needs of certainty that an anxiety sufferer craves so deeply (deleting pieces of information that don't fit with the programs). "Oh, how I long for the days when I could trust in uncertainty," the person thinks to themselves. How serious and deformed reality becomes, all for the sake of standing guard to a saber-toothed tiger that doesn't even exist.

An over-worrier tends to hold his or her breath or breathe very shallowly when experiencing something stressful. This is a big problem in the short term and the long term. Short term because your physiology controls your emotional state (the way you breathe and what posture you assume) and long term because every time the anxiety habits are continued, you get a little farther away from the true version of yourself. On the other hand, hyperventilation can result from expelling too much carbon dioxide too quickly, resulting in low levels of carbon dioxide in the blood. This can cause dizziness, depersonalization, belching, and many other reactions. Hyperventilation due to worry disrupts the natural balance between oxygen and carbon dioxide in the body, and the amygdala (responsible for the fight, flight, or freeze response) detects this instantly. Slow, deliberate breathing exercises send signals of safety to the amygdala, eventually leading to the restoration of inner harmony.

We'll be looking at the importance of controlling your emotional state through your physiology in later chapters; for now, just begin understanding how the addiction to suffering leads to the habit of worrying within the "I am" model.

3) Familiarity

Here's the golden rule that each of us unconsciously applies: If it's familiar, we move toward it; if it's not, we move away from it. No wonder anxiety sufferers are threatened by people who smile for no reason ("Why do they get to be so happy?"), or freak out the moment they don't feel the agitation that comes with their bodily symptoms of anxiety ("Where'd they go?"). What's familiar is safe, and what's unfamiliar is a threat. But how much of this unconscious program must we respect? And at what point in our lives must we start questioning our thoughts and feelings? How about now? Since waiting for the right time to commit to the change process will always lead to your mind coming up with more reasons for why you shouldn't, and why you'll never be able to maintain it. This is again an attempt by your system to maintain the patterns that you've already gotten good at and reject change of any kind.

Adopting an open mind is the key to reprogramming yourself and disengaging in this limiting cycle. When you open your mind up to new possibilities, life begins opening up to you as well. When a person has more options, they begin seeing through their limiting habits that have forced them into anxiety. Ask yourself whether many years down the road, lying on your deathbed, will you look back on your life and be proud of how comfortable your life was? Or would you rather look back and say I lived an exciting and creative life?

For most of us, familiarity doesn't lead to creativity; it leads to the lack of creativity. And we are creative geniuses deep within who are all longing for the opportunity to begin tapping into our unique abilities. Creativity is a function of the conscious mind, which leads to purpose, and you'll never find your purpose through familiarity. That's because with familiarity, you already know what to expect tomorrow, and next week, and next month, and years down the road should you choose to stay on the path you're on. And yes, it's a choice.

The current life system that pushes familiarity down our throats tells us that we must go to school, gain a good occupation, raise a family, save up for retirement, and die. What's creative about that? Does it make us virtuous and noble in some way to live like sheep? To succumb to what the world wants for us and to stay in line with the agendas of today's corporations? Here's another example of familiarity being propped up onto us. Have you ever heard the song "Work" by Rihanna? Do you know how many times the word "work" is repeated in that song? 82 times! Add the fact that you sing along to it and double that number, and now you're utilizing a skill set that the ancients brought to our attention called incantations and you're using it against yourself. Oh, how the cards are stacked against our anxiety healing if we continue keeping the door of our minds open to anyone who'd like to put anything in it. Without awareness, we are nothing. We are something, but that something isn't fulfilling, not even the least bit.

So, we understand the familiarity concept well, which fits into the "I am" model. We understand that bringing our awareness into play will open the doors to new options on how to perceive our internal ideas and external happenings. At this point, we also understand that we must choose between love and fear since every other feeling and emotion is an add-on to these two. If you choose love, you must choose unconditional love, starting with yourself and gently working on incorporating this attitude toward others. If you choose fear, you'll always be found wanting. You'll look toward moving to a new country for happiness, or getting a divorce and finding someone new; this hamster wheel of searching will never end.

Remember the morning mirror test from Chapter 2? You can also use it to determine whether love or fear is running your life. Look into the mirror within the first 15 minutes of waking up and describe what you see. Do you see progress and compassion, or do you see lack and hate? Be honest with yourself. Because within those first 15 minutes after waking, you'll learn everything you need to know that's currently stored within the deepest parts of you. This also brings us to the most important time of the day to begin breaking your limiting habits — the first 15 minutes. This is because you're moving from an unconscious state (sleeping) to a conscious state (awareness). This transition creates a shift in your brainwave patterns from a delta wave (deep sleep) state all the way to a beta wave (alert) state. This window of opportunity holds the key to an important part of the healing journey because the subconscious mind is more readily accessible during this transition, and during the time of going from unconscious to conscious. This is the reason for the enormous amount of content you see on binaural beats today. Since the belief is that listening to certain sound frequencies can help you gain access to the subconscious parts of you and affect different aspects of your life for the better (like sleep, concentration, and meditation). For me, the verdict is still out on how effective these binaural beats are.

Now, don't wake up and get frantic that what you do during this time will most likely dictate how your day goes; see it as a challenge. As we get deeper into this book, you'll begin tapping into exactly how to utilize the most powerful skillsets available toward healing your anxiety. Without a toolbox for healing that you can take with you throughout the day, you'll find yourself back in a distressed emotional state very quickly.

The biggest question in stage three of the "I am" model is can we move out of what's currently familiar that's causing us to gravitate toward inner distress, and move into a new familiar? The answer is yes. Because the power of neuroplasticity has shown us that we have the ability (at any age) to alter the neural connections that are currently firing and wiring in our brains. This capability puts us in a position to question everything about ourselves, and that is the key to freedom. As we question who we've become, why we unconsciously keep this character alive through secondary gains, and what future uncertainty keeps sabotaging our progress, we begin getting to know who we are. Right now, you really don't know who you are. The "you" you have become is the sum of thousands of people and their energetic influences, which have shaped you into the likeliness of them. That's familiarity, and that's what the world does. We've grown up thinking we need to compete with everyone and everything. Rarely do we feel a deep sense of pride toward others; instead, we conjure up thoughts and feelings of jealousy. It's the old "if I can't have it, no one can" attitude. It all comes back to familiarity.

4) Safety

The addiction to suffering leads to the habit of obsessively worrying; obsessively worrying leads to a sense of familiarity; and a sense of familiarity leads to feelings of safety. The subconscious mind has two goals: to keep us safe and to keep us happy. But if it has to choose between the two, it chooses safety every time; because if you're not safe, you run the risk of dying. If you die, you can't move your genes forward. The problem, though, is the system goes crazy! How else can you explain things like stoplights, a certain word you hear, or a color you see as being a trigger? Here are some other functions of the subconscious mind:

- It stores all your memories.
- It needs clear orders.
- It contains your instincts.
- It wants to automate everything.
- It thinks in pictures and takes things literally.

The fastest way to understand your present triggers is to investigate your past like a detective on a mission and recognize the experiences that can be placed into the category of emotional traumas. Many times, we can consciously recall these traumas because we stay stuck in a mood due to still hanging onto the same meaning over that event. This is because a mental snapshot is taken during the moment prior to the peak intensity of that experience, and then everything in that environment gets grouped and labeled as a threat. This pairing, or association, gets strengthened the more unconscious behaviors fall in line with the meaning of the event.

So let's dive deep into this question. If anxiety is a result of one or more previous experiences that led to a moment of "freezing" and helplessness, and our actions fall in line with the meanings over the reality that was placed during and after these past events, can we really blame ourselves for the creation of anxiety? Since these experiences are all a result of mechanisms within us that prioritize our survival over everything else, are we at fault? To me, the answer is both yes and no. Yes, it's our fault for not questioning how irrational these feelings and thinking patterns are, and for not taking action to alter them sooner. No, it's not our fault because the creation of this anxious state was largely out of our hands and exaggerated over time.

Either way, we have no time to stall. Stalling means strengthening anxiety. You must understand the roots of your anxiety and your resistance to change. Then analyze the formula that consistently puts you in an anxious place and begin the convincing game toward your subconscious once and for all. When you can see this journey through the understanding that it's a convincing game, you become more compassionate toward yourself in moments of feeling challenged (rather than berating yourself and placing blame). As you continue convincing your subconscious mind of how the old pairings are false and the new ones are true, safety begins getting placed on what's newly familiar since consistency is safety.

Before reading this book, I bet many of you never associated anxiety with safety. But now you know better. We unconsciously place the meaning of safety to our suffering. Suffering becomes a lifestyle, a potential opportunity for significance, as we gravitate toward other sufferers. The poor get poorer, the rich get richer, the happy ones get happier, the sad ones get sadder, and so on. This is no accident; it's a universal law. And the law of rhythm states that anything that is in rhythm with something will manifest more of that thing. Einstein

43

reminds us that the definition of insanity is doing the same thing and expecting a different result. So, take a good look into the "I am" model, recognize that you consciously and unconsciously got yourself into this pickle, and it's your responsibility to get yourself out of it. This is for the betterment of this world, which is waiting for your unique self to show up and teach people a thing or two, and for the sake of those who rely on you today.

5) I Am (Identity)

Many of the people who watch my YouTube videos and listen to my Anxiety Guy podcasts don't consciously realize the power behind the words I use at the end of each piece of content I create. Those words are "you are more than anxiety." These words sink below the level of conscious awareness until focus is turned toward them; they begin creating the internal shifts naturally. This phrase is a call for investigation, questioning, and passion. Investigation into how you developed into the "you" you are today, questioning into everything you believe about yourself and the things that cause you distress, and passion because of the dissatisfaction it conjures up. The last part is my favorite since it's the emotions that drive a person toward the first two. Being more than anxiety is basically like saying you aren't you; you may think you're you, and others may think you are you, but you aren't you. To overcome anxiety, you must begin disidentifying from the present you and begin identifying with a new and improved version. Not all parts of you in the present must disappear, though. You have personality traits that you want to keep, such as your problem-solving abilities, your patience, your hard-working style, your compassion, etc.

Keep what fits with the new identity and replace what doesn't fit.

Think about the journey like this:

Let's say you and me are good friends, and we've excelled at the sport of tennis up until now. All of a sudden, the tennis gods come down from the sky and say, "You can never play the sport of tennis again, but you may choose any other sport you'd like to excel in from this day forward." So, of course, your first thought is, "Damn, this is going to be hard. I've spent my whole life working on being the best tennis player I can be, and now I can't do it anymore!" Naturally, your next choice of sport would be one that involves a racquet or paddle, since this is a close second to tennis. But you stop yourself for a moment, and ask, "Is this my subconscious speaking?" Yes, I still have a sense of familiarity if I pick racquetball, for example. Yes, I'll be able to pick it up fast. And yes, this will make me feel good about myself again quickly. But what will I be missing by not committing to a whole new sport, like water polo, for example? I'll be missing out on working different body parts. I'll be missing out on meeting different types of people, and I'll be missing out on improving myself in something brand new.

This is also the case with shifting your "I am's" and, ultimately, your identity; you have to choose! Do you kind of want change and go for racquetball, or do you dive right in and embrace all the uncertainty that comes with committing to water polo? Let's not negate the fact that this kind of drastic change can come naturally to some, and be distressing (in the beginning) to most. The argument here is whether the change itself is the most difficult part, or is it your core beliefs around change that hold you back. I believe it comes down to your core beliefs more than it does the change itself. And as time goes by and you place yourself in more and more uncomfortable situations before they feel comfortable, this idea will become more real in your heart as well.

Having said that though, a long-term approach is always crucial. The last thing you want to become is one of those anxiety sufferers on the reassurance-seeking forums (RSFs), which is literally what most of them have turned into — people who get a temporary safety net by asking others whether they've suffered this or that. Not only that, these people believe that one tip, or one exercise, will release them from decades of repressed emotion and energy, paving the way to walk down that golden path to total healing. Stay clear of these groups and forums; you're in a transition toward becoming a warrior now — a warrior who senses the possibility of long-term change, a warrior who regards inner peace as true freedom, and a warrior who sees every challenge as an opportunity to move one step closer toward desensitization.

So, it's not who you are — you are more than anxiety — it's just things you're doing that lead to these feelings that you're experiencing. To begin moving toward a new identity, you need to have a clear vision of what that person is like:

- What is this person's general mindset when they take on the day?
- What is this person's situational mindset the moment an inner disruption shows up?

- What is the type of speed this person has adopted as they go about their day? Do they rush, or do they take their time, therefore having more access to thinking rather than just remembering and reacting?

We'll be diving deeper into all of this in future chapters. Right now, all you need to do is understand the "I am" formula fully before moving on to the next chapter, which comes down to:

The addiction to suffering (subconscious programs), which leads to...

Excessive worry (as worry provides you with something important that you may think you won't receive if you give up worrying), which leads to...

Familiarity (whatever came first and was practiced the most often becomes familiar), which leads to...

Safety (consistency = safety, and safety = higher chance of survival, therefore giving up safety is the greatest challenge).

Which finally leads to...

I Am. An identity, thinking you are what you think, speak, do, and imagine when it's just things you're doing.

Summary:

- If we dig deep enough, every anxiety sufferer has one or more secondary gains that keep them attached to anxiety. This secondary gain meets a need that in their minds may not get met once anxiety is overcome, and sabotages a person's progress.

- Anxiety, for the most part, isn't our fault, but it's our responsibility to put behind us once and for all.

- Worry may give you a sense of comfort and safety, but prevents you from seeing the big picture, and prevents your unique qualities from shining through.

- To overcome anxiety, 100% of you must be on board. This means congruency between the conscious and the subconscious mind, and it all starts with what you do within the first 15 minutes of waking up in the morning.

- Without a clear sensory-based vision for who you want to become, the seed will never get planted within your inner GPS to tap into the answers you seek. Generalities such as "I want to overcome anxiety," or "I just want to be happy," are too broad and not targeted enough. Instead, focus on how the future "you" thinks, how they express themselves, what power words they use the most, what habits are automatic in their life, how they view challenges, and what mindset they start with each day. These are just a few of the questions that will start the process toward becoming more than anxiety.

CHAPTER 4:

Uncovering The Threats

*"Never allow yourself to be carried
away by your first impressions."*

In today's society, we are bombarded with fearful messages that form more and more connections to threats in the outside world. On paper, many of these threats (which activate the fight, flight, or freeze response) seem tame at best. It's not important to note how these threats look on paper but instead recognize the underlying reason it affects us so deeply. When I discuss threats, I'm certainly not talking about life or death situations, but words and some actions by others, scenarios, and environments.

When it comes to threats that unnecessarily activate a person's stress response, the most important ones are threats to the identity — who they believe they are and the qualities they bring to the world. People form an identity of themselves by about the age of 7. The identity isn't labeled as good or bad to the great protector of your core belief system known as your critical factor. Instead, it's like a sacred diamond that needs protection from any invaders that may have the intention of stealing it.

A person's identity gets strengthened as time goes on, and anything that denies the continuation of the identity gets rejected. Sometimes, even positivity by others is seen as a threat, and jealousy may arise (a clear sign of a violation of a person's way of being). This usually occurs at an unconscious level — people with certain identities usually gravitate toward people with similar identities. Depressed people hang out with other depressed people; optimistic people hang out with optimistic people, and so on. When it comes to these threats, we may not understand why we react the way we do, and might even beat ourselves up for being so pessimistic. However, at a deeper level, if pessimism was the consistent message early on, and it fed into the emotional cycle you regularly felt, it becomes a part of your identity. Here are a few of the threats (you may or may not be aware of) that may be running your life right now:

Threats to parenting (especially mothers)

Mothers carry their babies for 9 months and are usually the primary caregiver through a child's early years. Dad, more often than not, comes and goes into the picture. Mom and dad believe they do a lot for their children, as they sacrifice what they need to in order to bring up their child in a well-balanced way. So when a parent is confronted with a scenario that challenges the positive beliefs that the parent holds about bringing up their child, the stress response can get activated. It's a threat to what they believe they earned; the right to call themselves a good parent. If a situation arises that opposes this belief, it can feel similar to having a car just barely scrape you without getting hit. The parent's heart rate increases, they start sweating excessively, and their stomach gets tight, all in the hopes of getting the parent out of there or fight back the threat.

One of the shakiest periods in a parent's life is when a school teacher calls a meeting. The child does something that goes against the school rules, and the parent is forced to face the firing squad, multiple disgruntled teachers with white lights shining brightly in the face of mom (or dad). OK, the teachers may not be disgruntled, nor are there any shiny white lights, but that's sure what it feels like before arriving at the meeting. During the meeting, all the parent can think about is "I'm such a bad parent. I suck. I screw everything up. I can't even parent my own child." The parent has their values threatened in a big way and begins distorting the words of others to match their threatened emotions. Words should never be able to negatively affect a person; it just shouldn't happen. But we live in a world where words can hurt as much as rocks can, sometimes much worse.

The physical body

Someone who places great importance on the way they look, spending years at the gym molding themselves into the perfect specimen can also be easily caught off guard. If they're at the gym and notice a person with an inch more on their biceps or a more symmetrical physique, all of a sudden the stress response becomes activated. They feel the threat in a similar way that our ancestors did back in the day when two men fought for the love of a woman. The man who won the fight (usually the stronger one) got the girl, and the other lost his chance at love. This, again, is directly connected to what the person believes is connected to their identity, physical strength, and many times, good looks. The threat can even come from someone asking, "Why do your shoulders look weaker than your back?" The person immediately labels themselves as small, weak, and incapable of improvement. The conscious mind knows better than to take on the opinions of others, but the subconscious mind, which has believed for a long time that physical strength and looks make a man (or woman), is threatened and so the internal safety alarm gets activated.

Social status

In today's world, losing your reputation can feel like a life-or-death scenario. A rumor in your community about you must be contained as soon as possible, or you may feel you have to find a new life in another city. In the old days, we had tribes that we could rely on in case some external threat, like invading tribes or animals, threatened our lives. The bigger our tribe, the more likely we could deal with the incoming threat to our lives; the smaller the tribe, the less chance for our survival. This mentality still exists today, but now the threat is ideas and opinions. We work to please others so they keep us as friends, and we look to grow these circles larger and larger due to our tribe mentality. The moment someone in our circle (or even outside of our circle) defies us and places their negative opinion over us, our stress response kicks in.

Words like "you're not good enough," or "you're fired," can send a shockwave of emotions that can potentially cause us to freeze at that moment helplessly. In reality, these are just opinions and judgments from others. They shouldn't have the power to affect us on the inside, and yet they do because, in this case, we hold others up on a pedestal. We feel the need to fight for people's attention because we got so little of it from our authority figures when we were young, and that void needs filling. Our sanity hangs by a thread as we cling to every word that other people say. What slavery, what vulnerability. If only we saw the truth, that the right people will come into our lives at the right time — we don't need to become so affected by people's opinions and words. Everybody's got an opinion, they're the cheapest things in the world, and most of those opinions are due to their own unfinished business from their emotionally traumatic past.

Once I stopped taking things personally, I started to see things from the perspective of the other person's child side that still lived within their adult bodies. Their body had grown, but their mentality and emotional state never changed. I was the victim of their repressed emotions and upbringing for far too long, and once I put these moments of clarity together, I gave up on any kind of social status I would have clung to years back. You can do the same. Even if the worst happens, and you get fired at work, to take that to a personal level is absurd. It's a job; you still have all your limbs in place, a fully functional brain, and yet we acknowledge that the activation of our stress response is the truth by feeding ourselves the dumbest stories like:

"I'll never get another job, and I'll be homeless."

"Everyone hates me."

"My spouse will leave me."

53

Helplessness comes so naturally to us these days. But I'll tell you what, you'll get another job, no one hates you (and even if they did that's their problem), and if your spouse is with you because of your career, it's probably best that he or she leaves for the sake of your future self. Try explaining that logically to your subconscious mind, though, and you'll get a whole lot of resistance since you've been conditioned already for years to place great emphasis on your social status. However, the recognition of how these beliefs no longer serve you in your adult life is a key step toward changing them in time.

Questioned health

It's not uncommon for people to be concerned about their health, but this is taken to a whole new level by today's health-anxiety sufferers. Understandably, the stress response gets triggered by real threats to our physical body, but some people are sent into a frenzy when they hear someone else say something like, "You don't look so good," early in the morning. A person who believes they are in mediocre health won't become as emotionally riled up by any threat to their mental, emotional, or physical health. Mediocre health is already a part of their identity; it's who they are. However, someone who prides themselves on good health can curse themselves and the world while experiencing the full throttle of fight, flight, or freeze almost instantly should they be met with an opposing perspective. This is what the media thrives on; by getting you into a constant state of fear, they control you since anyone who controls another person's emotions controls how they think and what they do. So we become bombarded by news of death, struggle, and illness keeping us on our toes and having us connect it to who we are. We begin placing limits on how long we will live and what we're capable of as we grow old since that's the message we hear the most often. It's frustrating because we place such importance on what we hear and see, rather than our own unique experiences. If only we began realizing the immense capability of our minds, emotions, and physical bodies to heal and paid little-to-no respect toward another person's personal experience, or the media, we'd live a long and fulfilling life. Yet, we become fragile at a moment's notice when we should remember that one person's experience isn't our own, and the agendas of the media don't have to be fulfilled through us.

Sporting events

The more obsessed you are with your favorite sports team, the more you'll be met with your stress response. When watching a soccer game, for example, as the opposing team gets closer and closer to your favorite team's goal, you may feel as if your kids are being threatened with their lives. Your emotions go up when your team scores, and down when they get scored on causing you to become an emotional yo-yo. You then bring that emotional roller coaster into each aspect of your life and look for instant gratification in all you do, never committing to anything for the long term. This threat that activates the stress response seems harmless, but it can become addictive since it also holds within it the opportunity to release some of the emotional charge that's been stored within a person's body due to past traumas. They feel better when they're up and down, a sense that they can release their repressed emotion, only to realize that the void leftover from their past never seems to lift fully. The problem lies within the experiences of the past and not with the opposing sports team, although many fans unconsciously see the opposing team in the same way they view the person who neglected them, threatened them, or beat them in their past. It's not dad; it's just a friendly human wearing opposing colors. You need to deal with dad and stop taking out your rage on the opposition. I, for example, used to live in this emotional rollercoaster. I began placing less emphasis on my team winning the game, and more on enjoying the strengths of both sides. I became more of a neutral observer rather than a frantic sports hooligan. The key here is to check in with yourself from time to time — to observe yourself from the outside and see whether the actions that are attached to your emotions are supportive or not. If not, the transition must begin.

Fear of failure

Welcome to a large majority of my past life. With every "mistake" I made that didn't satisfy my authority figures, the more I felt like a failure. This led me to avoidance behaviors in the hope of staying within my comfort zone. The fear of failure can be worse than the actual "failure" itself, leaving a person in a constant fight, flight, or freeze state. Everything a person does gets matched with their low level of capability they believe they have, and the need to maintain daily routine overtakes the desire to act differently. Reframing the past (we'll get to that in future chapters) in order to bring up new perceptions over those events releases the need to do things a certain way. As the fear of failure gets released, so does the need to try to control things that are out of our control. The stress response no longer becomes activated through the anticipation of failure, and instead, the future experience is seen through an open mind that welcomes any result that shows up. There's no failure, only feedback. Remind yourself that going for what you truly want will lead to a reconnection with your higher self. This higher self knows no irrational fear and commits to the process of taming the stress response at the core.

Uncertainty

The thought of meeting new people, moving to a new location, walking on a new path, trying a new dish, trying on different clothes, or any other unfamiliar act can send a person straight toward the stress response. Anxiety sufferers resist uncertainty as much as they can, which gives them very few new life experiences. As they grow older, they begin to realize how much they've missed out on simply because they continued moving toward certainty and away from uncertainty. There must be new clarity that arises from this as a result, though. Since the uncertain act itself isn't the trigger but instead the association to the action that might be taken, we can begin placing new meanings over that uncertain action. Daredevils take this to a whole new level and live for the thrill of uncertainty; anxiety sufferers are the complete opposite. I'm glad to be right in the middle of both. There's a Tibetan proverb that preaches the will to live a single day like a tiger over living a thousand years as a sheep. That tiger was once a cub that also faced much uncertainty and proved his inner doubts wrong, and became a powerful tiger, just as you will be as you understand and apply the RIC teachings in this book.

Summary:

- Most of the time, the stress response is a reaction to a perceived threat, not a real one.

- What you deem as threatening is just different; there's no threat in it, only the fact that uncertainty lies within it.

- The opinions of others are based on factors such as their own emotional state, their upbringing, their belief system, and many other factors. To take them as truth is to let the world dictate who you are and what you're capable of.

- Turning an imagined threat into safety requires a shift in perception. For this shift in perception to show up, certain past events that still cause you a deep, "icky" feeling must be reframed, and responding in the moment of irrational fear must be implemented consistently. This two-part process is the key to interpreting your world in a safe manner.

- You've never failed, you've only gained lessons and feedback, and now you can use those lessons to develop into the greatest version of you.

CHAPTER 5:

Where I Went Wrong During My Recovery

"Stop under-valuing yourself, and over-valuing everyone else."

Do I regret that I went through a debilitating, medically diagnosed anxiety disorder for 6 years (without the diagnosis, it was closer to 27 years)? No. It made me who I am today. It gave me a purpose in life, which was the chance to contribute positively toward other people. It taught me lessons I couldn't have learned anywhere else. I have no regrets whatsoever. However, there were some things I believed, and did, that kept me from healing anxiety much faster. Because it's never the lack of knowledge or tools, or enough support by others either, it's always our core beliefs around healing that hold us back. For me, it was like having a jet pack strapped to my back and an anchor strapped to my waist. The more willpower I asserted, and progress I made, the longer the drag from the anchor. You can see this conflict between the conscious mind and habit in many people going through anxiety today.

Once I was able to cut the anchor by renegotiating my past traumas — as well as questioning my core beliefs (subconscious beliefs) and turning my newfound clarity from a thought level to a heart level — I was fully ready for healing.

Here's what kept me from lasting change:

Taking advice from people who weren't that good at giving advice (bless their hearts)

What you believe about your potential to heal mainly comes down to the people you surround yourself with the most. I surrounded myself with people who said they cared, but they never took the time to pick up a book on anxiety (this is not meant to blame, but to learn and adjust). Therefore, their advice wasn't eye-opening or practical, and it kept me digging deeper into my ditch of inner helplessness. I was looking for the answers on the outside, and not listening to the real answers when they showed up on the inside. This is kind of the same as when someone has a tremendous moment of progress, only to remind themselves that the good feelings don't fit in with who they believe they are. So, they go right back to being anxious again, forgetting the positive experience and denying the "aha" moment of clarity that came with it.

The more I blamed them, the less I blamed myself. Two birds, one stone! If I blamed myself anymore, I was headed down the very real possibility of committing suicide. I had to offload some of this suppressed energy somehow. Looking for advice from people who've never gone through what you have, and have come out on the other side, is a lose-lose situation. You're losing because you're moving farther away from the answers that are within you, and you're getting feedback that isn't practical. How can you possibly use advice like "just stop thinking about it," or "just let it go"? You can't. I almost strangled my good friend Mike because he kept saying, "It's all in your head," one too many times. I would respond, "If it's in my head, Michael, how do I get this goddamned idea OUT of my head, hmmm?!" To which he'd say, "Learn to relax." I loved the guy, but I had to distance myself from him because I knew I had to do this on my own before reconnecting again.

Never give up your autonomy; it's challenging to get it back. Your identity is yours to design; it's no one else's job. And people who know nothing about anxiety should never be put in a position to advise an anxiety sufferer. It's like asking a professional dart player to tell you what to do in basketball. They're worlds apart! This means that we are also to blame for relying on people who clearly don't understand the journey. The support people in your life have taken you as far as they can. They can't take you any farther, and they can't guide you any better (unless it comes from their heart to look much deeper into your targeted challenges). What you really need is to surround yourself with like-minded warriors: those people who are currently on the journey of healing anxiety or have completed the process and are now in maintenance mode (applying habits that maintain their neutral-to-pleasant emotional states).

You've probably heard the saying, "you become the five people you spend the most time with," and there's plenty of truth behind it. There are just as many anxiety success stories out there as there are victim stories. The only challenge is it takes a little more digging online or offline to find these people. Take The Anxiety Guy Facebook Page and Group, for example. There are set rules that state only questions toward healing, progress reports that you're proud of, discussions about recent content, and optimistic communication between members are allowed. You can't *not* heal in a place like this. You literally have no choice, because every time you grab a silly idea from the sky that leads to fear and worry, you can't just outlet it on these pages. You are now forced to do something you've never been trained to do, think. You must think your way past the inner challenge, therefore imagining your way to a new possibility, prior to acting on it to cement the meaning you just created. If an idea stays as an idea, it can't harm you or lift you up. If an idea is led toward a spiderweb effect, therefore growing more possibilities behind the idea and leading to emotions that are in line, it's going to affect your perceptions and actions. These are the building blocks that lead to your life metaphor. For some, life is a "never-ending dark tunnel," and for others, life is "a pleasant and natural ride through a canal."

A person who understands the journey, responds practically, and stimulates your imagination in a more positive direction is like finding gold. You don't need dozens of truly supportive people in your life, in fact, I suggest against it, or else you'll find yourself addicted to needing feedback from others.

Thinking that recovery would take the same amount of time as it took for me to develop anxiety

For a long time, I thought it would take years to overcome anxiety. It took years to develop this mess, so it must take years to heal, right? Wrong. This is why you see so many people give up on themselves. They believe they're "in too deep" and they live with beliefs like "you can't teach an old dog new tricks." This is another sign of the need for control, the demise of every anxiety sufferer today. The action of trusting in uncertainty fills them with dread, and so they revert to what's easy, suffering.

I remember telling myself that I'm going to just start doing the inner work and see where it leads me. I began feeling better, and this time believed I deserved to leave the addiction to suffering and my anxious identity behind, and in time, healing arrived. As I mentioned earlier, healing doesn't mean that you cross a finish line, and angels come floating down around you with trumpets. It means you keep at the inner work because your transition is never complete. You heard that right. You don't have the luxury to entertain even one irrational or pessimistic idea because if you do, you might fall back into the cycle of anxiety again.

It's like checking your website now and then to make sure everything's working properly, and upgrading it constantly toward the desires of today's search engines. In this example, the website is your beliefs, identity, and purpose, and the search engine is God. Depending on what you believe, who you believe you are, and what you believe you deserve, as well as whether you're fulfilling your true purpose in this world, you'll either be in line with source energy or out of line. If you're in line, you have graduated toward a higher state of consciousness and to living in a flow state — the state of natural connectedness to everything pure in this world. If you're out of line with source energy, your life will come with daily raging battles on the inside and on the outside.

The timeframe for your healing is out of your hands. You can only take control of what you have control over that will give you the best chance for a quick transition. Never allow yourself to judge your progress day by day. It's not helpful to think "today was a good day because I had no anxiety," or "today was a bad day because I had that moment of anxiety when I woke up, even though the rest of the day was fine, it's still a bad day." Oh, the perfectionism, the internal pressure; no wonder you feel like a volcano that is ready to erupt the next opportunity you get. You're never pleased, you don't know yourself well enough, and you're scared of bringing out the information from your past emotional traumas that are keeping you stuck. Without depth, you'll never heal, period.

I had to reframe (I'll explain reframing in detail later) dozens of past memories, and effectively respond to hundreds of catastrophic thoughts during my healing journey. In the beginning, it was like walking through a dark forest with no one around me. For a long time, I did everything in my power to stuff aside those "bad" memories or visions for my future. I worked out harder, I drank, I took Ativan, and I even became a shopaholic. Not because I enjoyed any of those things tremendously, it was because all I ever knew was to run from my problems. I hadn't been taught how to deal with my inner challenges. Commercials, my friends, and advertising told me it was OK to deal with them in this way, so I did. Go to any workout gym in your community and look around at the people there. Are any of them smiling? Do any of them look excited to be doing what they're doing? Almost none! They're all running from themselves and taking a brief opportunity to discharge stored energy that's been eating away at them for the better part of their lives. If you don't take control of what you have control over, the world will take control of you.

Thinking that it was universal law not to change my core beliefs and who I was from my childhood. Thinking it was a show of disrespect and a sign of disconnection from my authority figures.

For years I walked around with an icky feeling when it came to positive change. Unconsciously I believed that my relationship with my parents and other authority figures was due to what we had in common. In this case, it was worry and anxiety. Letting go of this filled me with tremendous guilt. How could I possibly live with myself if I was free and my dad wasn't (dad had an anxiety disorder for decades, and is in maintenance now)? Beyond the guilt, I would be denying generations of anxious habits in my family. Funny how, when dad started to feel consistent mental, emotional, physical, and spiritual relief during my early 30s, I also was beginning my personal transition to freedom from anxiety. It was like getting permission before I could truly heal. Consciously I never recognized this until years later; what a wake-up call that was.

I'm a big believer that it's not necessarily the thoughts we think that contribute to who we become, but the thoughts that we entertain and give priority to. Most of the thoughts we think aren't even ours; they're the ideas of others. It's not our voice we hear in our heads and reacting in our bodies; it's theirs. But do we take the time to dive deeper into this new realization for the betterment of ourselves? Sometimes, not nearly enough, because we feel like we'll lose something and never get it back again. We walk around as a carbon copy of others who've come and gone in our lives; the only difference is we look a little different. Everything else, from our thinking styles, to our verbal language to our behaviors and even our religious and spiritual beliefs are the same. And we're supposed to be unique, beautifully different in every which way from the next person.

I want you to know this right now: Moving away from your parents' beliefs doesn't mean you love them less. It just means that you're ready for maturation, the process of growing out of your limited belief systems from childhood. Life is change. If you're not evolving, it means you're stuck in the same experiences from your past. And if you get stuck with the same experiences from your past, it means that you're repeatedly reliving your emotional traumas (most likely at a lesser emotional degree). If you want new experiences, you must begin questioning everything, and I mean everything. When I did an inventory of my core beliefs, I couldn't believe how much garbage was in there. How did I allow myself to live with these beliefs for so long, I wondered? I quickly realized how the brain seeks efficiency. It doesn't want to relearn things repeatedly. It loves habit; it likes you the way you are, hence the resistance to positive change — what a massive eye-opener.

Thinking That If I Overcame One Inner Challenge or Disorder, My Life Would Be All Better

Not so fast warrior. Overcoming that one symptom of anxiety, or that one situation, or that one thought that repeatedly plays out in your mind won't make suffering go away forever in most cases. It's the subconscious programs that become the core of your emotional distress. And this worrying habit would find its way into another aspect of your life almost instantly. It's like playing the classic '80s video game Q*Bert (I loved that game). Q*Bert jumps from one square to the next looking to pick up bonus items. Think of this as your subconscious trying to group more things related to fear together. Its job is to avoid enemies. In this case, it's anything that goes against your subconscious programs, even things like self-love since it opposes the fear-based programs. But what happens when Q*Bert runs out of squares? Does the game end? No, it doesn't, he just starts all over at the top of the screen. This deeper part of you looks to fulfill the earliest known connections it has made between things, the pairings, so when one fear is no longer an issue, another reason for sensitivity shows up.

This is why so many people become agoraphobic (afraid of open spaces, crowded areas). They lock themselves in their house because, over time, these connections between the brain and body have made it seem like the saber-toothed tiger is everywhere. Just as our ancestors did by hiding out in caves, so do we hide out in our comfort zones. This is related to the reptilian brain, which picks up sensory information. This is prior to relaying the information it picks up to the emotional brain, or limbic system. Once the situation gets to a certain level of heightened emotion, the third major part of the brain called the neocortex (the thinking, rationalizing, analyzing brain) has no chance of having a say as we automatically avoid the external stimuli at all costs. Smaller and smaller our world becomes, and the more and more disconnected we feel. No wonder so many anxiety sufferers believe they're going crazy or will lose control at any moment. All they have to do is look around and realize how wrong their version of reality is.

But we're not here to play the helpless victim anymore, you've picked up this book because you're dissatisfied with the present version of who you are, and you're ready to start living. To start living, we must tackle anxiety at its root and stop believing that coping and managing the thoughts and feelings is as good as it gets. F**ck coping!

In order to heal from anxiety, it's essential that you wake up each day expecting internal and external challenges to show up. Many anxiety sufferers wake up feeling decent and begin praying to the anxiety gods not to show up on that day. How well does this work? It doesn't. Because a strategy based around hoping, trying, and wishing will leave you powerless. When you get to the point of feeling powerless, you begin feeling hopeless, and when you become hopeless, you may become agoraphobic. Bruce Lee said it beautifully when he said, "Be like water." A river doesn't stop flowing when it's met with a log; it takes a slight detour and keeps on the path it's on. A flow state is to be like water, and it doesn't mean that at every turn you'll be met with rainbows and unicorns. Life is challenging, and it's what we choose to do, and how we respond to those challenges that ultimately decides our future.

Thinking that i had to 'believe in myself' before i could heal

A big moneymaker is going around the self-help world today, and that moneymaker is the phrase, "you have to believe in yourself." I call bullshit and loads of it. Belief hardly ever shows up at the beginning of a new journey, it's developed as you go through the journey. How can you possibly believe in something you've never done before? There's no history of success around it, and if something isn't familiar, it will always be questioned at first. This idea alone, which can get plugged into an anxiety sufferer's mind, is enough to turn them away from healing. They become demoralized because they think, "If I don't believe in myself, I'll never be able to maintain healing for the long term, so why bother?" This was me for a very long time until I looked a little closer into all the things I excelled at in my life, only to realize that in time, and with momentum, came inner belief.

At the beginning of the healing journey over anxiety, a person must have an understanding of the proper mindset that will keep them moving forward and not avoid but overcome the blips along the way. A person must have skillsets to be able to counter certain internal challenges like intrusive thoughts, physical symptoms, or emotionally intense moments. We'll be going deep into these and other important aspects necessary for healing anxiety later in the book. For now, put away the idea that you must believe in yourself, and just start getting your feet wet with the world of uncertainty.

Believing that i had to will myself through anxiety each day, and fight through it all

We live in a world where we seem to fight everything. We fight when we protest, we fight cancer, we fight to get ahead in our career, we fight through traffic, we fight to get to the head of the line, and we fight past anxiety. If your current strategy for getting to a better mental, emotional, and physical place is to fight for it, you're going to make things worse before you make them better (as your current results are showing you). This is because willpower is a finite resource, and you only have a limited amount of it.

When you wake up each morning, you have a certain number of willpower points. That number depends on many things: how much sleep you got (as well as the amount of REM sleep), how many small decisions you have to make upon waking, and your blood sugar levels (please eat breakfast). Let's say you start your day with a total of 30 willpower points because you did all the right things before getting into your car and driving to work. If you're in the car and deciding on what type of music to play and it's taking you longer than you expected, 4 willpower points are taken away. If you begin thinking of all the things that could go wrong at work, another three willpower points are taken away. If someone cuts you off on the road and you show him the middle finger and say the words that would make your mother cringe, you've lost another 8 willpower points. Suddenly, you're at work and only have 15 of your 30 willpower points left. Once 2 p.m. rolls around, you're pretty much out of points, you've hit the wall, you need a nap, and you've turned yourself into an unconscious robot going through the motions.

A lack of willpower points is why it's so easy for people to succumb to a fearful idea. A thought is just a thought, but if you're out of willpower points, you won't have the capacity to question the thought. And so, the anxious cycle begins (and many times ends by leaving the hospital with all physical tests coming out negative). There's no fuel left in the tank, and the only way to put more in, so that you can begin utilizing your thinking brain again, is through rest, sleep, or food. If you don't refuel with rest, sleep, or food, your decision-making fails, and then guilt and blame get strengthened; you are at the mercy of the world's suggestions. You get home with 0 willpower points and head straight to the fridge, looking for the tallest beer and greasiest pizza. At around 10 or 11 p.m., you get a second wind, and you stay up longer because you now refer to yourself as a "night owl," and the whole process shows up again the next day. Welcome to the process of disintegration.

As your attitude of "fight through everything" gets strengthened, your sympathetic system is always activated (fight, flight, or freeze) while your parasympathetic system never gets to show up (rest and digest). No wonder a person's perceptual filters get so distorted, and they start assuming they're in danger all the time. Fighting is the opposite of allowing and inner peace. But how can someone meet with inner peace if they've never experienced it before? They will get flustered when it shows up, they won't know what to do with themselves, and quickly find something to worry about and fight over again. Again, welcome to the addiction to suffering. And how can one accept the feelings, thoughts, and sensations without the tools to do so. Therefore, I have a problem with people telling you that all you have to do is "accept" it. You can't accept until you understand, you can't understand until you alter your thinking, and you can't alter your thinking if you have no willpower points because you'll just revert back to anxious reactions.

Have you noticed that many of today's influencers seem emotionally balanced as they go about their day? They don't miss a beat; their minds work for them, they're in a flow state. Take former President Barack Obama, for instance. He understood the theory of willpower depletion very well (he only wore black and blue suits during his presidency, which resulted in less time deciding and more willpower points). Another example is Mark Zuckerberg, CEO of Facebook. He wears the same colored and styled shirt almost every day because, again, he understands that if he spends less time making small decisions, he'll have more energy to handle the challenges and bigger decisions as his day progresses. Your conscious mind is only as powerful as the number of willpower points you have in the tank. This is a big reason Jeff Bezos, founder of Amazon, makes all his big daily decisions in the morning, and also when he plans his most important meetings.

Reprogramming the subconscious mind is done by directly communicating with it (as we'll understand better later on in this book), but also by strengthening the conscious mind. Think about it; you've got a greasy guy (your intrusive thoughts, your physical symptoms, your emotional distress) dancing with your wife, would you just sit back and watch? Of course not, because the longer they dance with each other, the more rapport they'll build with each other. Just like the longer your current core beliefs, thinking patterns, and identity stick around, the stronger they become. What you would do in this situation is to find a way to get in the way. To do something to break up the dance. In this case, to break up the momentum built up by these negative habits.

So understand that you can replace fighting for freedom with flowing toward freedom. Healing should come naturally and effortlessly as you put the puzzle pieces together that eventually form a brand-new personality within.

Thinking that this struggle with anxiety is solely related to a 'mental disorder'

People out there believe that if they can just change their thinking, they'll be free, but the truth is that your anxiety goes much deeper than that. It started early on between the ages of 0-5, and changing your thinking alone might not alter your perceptions over your traumatic memories, your emotional state, and your core beliefs. Yes, to heal from anxiety we must alter our thinking, but we must also give ourselves permission to feel a certain neutrality during certain situations. We must reframe the scary images in our head that relate to past experiences so that we can imagine a future free from anxiety in all aspects of life. We must also build up our faith in the unknown, God, nature, and source energy if we are going to learn how to trust in uncertainty and stop looking to control everything.

I think it's shortsighted to place an anxiety sufferer in the "mental disorder" category without taking the time to dig deeper. Why else do we see such little improvement in individuals doing long-term talk therapy, and many even getting worse than after they started? That's years of trying to talk your way past anxiety only to find yourself broke, frustrated, and overwhelmed. You can't blame today's first-line treatments though, if you went through that much rigorous schooling, you'd be pretty close-minded too. There would be no spiritual component to healing and I can tell you this from experience, every anxiety sufferer who finds freedom finds themselves in a deep awakening at some point in the journey; a place where they feel a rebirth occurring, and a place where they start to understand the lessons from all their suffering better. You don't get here only by analyzing and thinking. Yes, thinking your way past sticky situations is important, but you get here by trusting, consciously imagining, and tapping into the resources already hidden within you. This is a big reason why so many people find healing through meditation these days. It's the meditation, the ability to be one with the discomfort and inner distress, that teaches us the lessons we need to learn to move past it. Meditation is a tool, an experience that leads to clarity; this clarity wasn't thought up but showed up when you least expected it. So, let's begin peeling back the layers of your anxiety through this book. Let's approach it with an open mind as we question your current formula for coping.

Summary:

- Stop placing your hopes on people who've never gone through what you have; it's empty advice.
- Understand that there's no timeline for your recovery. Everyone recovers at their own speed, and the less pressure you put on yourself to heal, the faster you will heal.
- You are allowed to oppose what you've been taught is the truth about you, and this world.
- Worry is a habit, and since everything evolves and changes, so must our habits.
- You need to be relentless in your pursuit of small daily wins over anxiety. Belief in yourself grows

over time, and most likely won't be there at the beginning of the journey.

- The imagination is far more powerful than willpower; begin learning how to imagine consciously, rather than imagine unconsciously, therefore leading you to believe in the catastrophic outcome.
- There's much more here than just calling anxiety a mental disorder. Throughout this book, we will unpack these components, and through understanding and daily application, we will meet with personal freedom.

CHAPTER 6:

The 8 Laws of Anxiety Recovery

"We are everywhere other than where we are right now, and therein lies the biggest problem."

I have studied thousands of anxiety success stories over the years and realized that healing from anxiety doesn't happen by accident. The people who succeed either transferred the necessary qualities from one aspect of their lives toward their anxiety healing or they relentlessly practiced attaining these traits to set themselves up for success. As we dive deep into the eight laws of anxiety recovery, I want you to ask yourself where you currently stand with each one. Will you need to work on attaining some of them, or can you already identify them in other aspects of your life? If you already have acquired these traits, ask yourself what may be holding you back from applying them toward healing anxiety.

Law #1 – The Law Of Optimism

A key ingredient in your healing will be you tapping into the successful outcome of your efforts to heal anxiety for good. Optimism is a human superpower — some people have it, and others have to work at it. Optimism might be difficult to see externally, but on the inside, an optimistic person has a sense that everything will turn out the way the conscious mind desires it to be. Optimistic people fight less and trust more. They know that if they do the right things each day, eventually what they want will manifest. To give you an example of the opposite of optimism, which is pessimism, I can look back on my days living with anxiety. I convinced myself that it would take me the same amount of time to heal as I had suffered. I limited myself, and everything I could do, based on my age (I wasn't even that old), and I took everything personally, which only fed into my pessimism.

Starting today, you have every reason to grow your optimism toward your healing. This is due to new studies coming out within the field of neuroscience that point to the brain being incredibly neuroplastic. Neuroplasticity is the brain's ability to form new synaptic connections in response to learning. This translates into good news for you since you picked up this book, are studying it and gaining the clarity needed, and allowing the change process to show up effortlessly. When I mean effortlessly, I don't say sit on your butt all day after reading this book and make no changes in your life. I mean sensing that everything is coming together as you learn and gently apply the teachings daily.

One study on optimism was conducted by a group of scientists from Boston and Harvard University who evaluated 1,306 men with an average age of 61. Each volunteer was evaluated for an optimistic or pessimistic style as well as for blood pressure, cholesterol, obesity, smoking, alcohol use, and family history of heart disease.

None of the men had been diagnosed with coronary artery disease when the study began. Over the next 10 years, the most pessimistic men were more than twice as likely to develop heart disease than the most optimistic men, even after taking other risk factors into account. Over 600,000 people in North America die every year due to heart disease. Could it be that an optimistic approach to life could have made a difference in their outcome? And if so, imagine the possibilities for you on your healing journey through anxiety.

Law #2 – The Law Of Reframing

In this book, I debated whether to combine reframing (imagery-based healing methods to reframe memories) and responding (effective cognitive, auditory, and physiological responses in the moment of fear) together or keep them separate. I decided to separate the two so as not to confuse you. Reframing without responding limits progress, and so does responding without reframing. They both need to be practiced daily for maximum benefit. But focusing on the law of reframing, we must understand the significance it holds toward our abilities to adopt a new identity for ourselves. Reframing places the person back into power over their lives. It creates a gray area to fill in new beliefs about things in the outside world and new beliefs about who the person is and what they are capable of. Prior to reframing, a person is placed under many limits over their potential in all aspects. This is due to the dozens, if not hundreds, of brains of others that have filled the person with ideas around who they are and what reality is really like. After reframing, life gets much lighter, the struggle seems to pass slowly, and everything seems positively different. Reframing is a skill that gets stronger over time. The stronger this skill becomes, the more absorbed in the imagery-based experience you become. The more absorbed you become, the more you allow your emotions to reveal themselves through crying, yawning, or other ways of emotional discharge.

Law #3 – The Law Of Momentum

Let's say a person is having a very anxious morning, and then a much larger problem shows up in the afternoon. They won't have access to all of their inner capabilities to think and act in ways that can solve the problem. However, if a person is having a neutral or even pleasant morning and a problem shows up in the afternoon, they'll have a much better chance of seeing the big picture and knowing how to deal with it. For an anxiety sufferer to be able to reach their emotional goals, they must get to the point of boredom and disinterest over their past limiting beliefs and thoughts. This becomes very hard to accomplish if the person doesn't gather up small wins throughout the day. A win can be anything from responding to a challenging situation with a new perception, to speaking with someone in a less helpless manner, or to taking a more empowered approach and responding in defiance to your irrational fears. There are also big wins that favor the law of momentum. Things you never thought you could think, say, do, or imagine show up after tremendous dissatisfaction with anxiety, and a feeling of tremendous accomplishment comes over you. Either way, pay attention to your small wins; they are the building blocks to your new identity.

Law #4 – The Law Of Clarity

Every epiphany that runs past your mind must be held onto, even written down. I love the idea of a clarity journal and advise many of my clients to start one. Without consciously looking for it, knowing you've done great reframing and responding work lately, you run into a tremendous moment of clarity. Maybe you wore something funny to the mall, and no one cared, maybe you said something in a crowd that you thought everyone would laugh at, and they loved it, maybe you sparked a conversation with a stranger while your physical symptoms were present and they never noticed. The clarity gained from these experiences goes right into your clarity journal to alert the subconscious mind of the facts that connect to the new beliefs you're beginning to adopt. A moment of clarity doesn't even have to appear because you did something; it can show up anytime, which doesn't mean it's less important than after a change in behavior. It's just as important, so write it down.

The more clarity you gain, the easier it will be to respond and challenge your limited thinking. No longer is your mindset "I'll try this and hope it works," it's more like "I'm starting to see things in this way naturally now, and it's becoming more real by the day." The law of clarity will lead to strengthening the power of your conscious mind because the more clarity that's gained, the more aware and analytical you become (analytically balanced, of course). You begin finding yourself pausing before reacting, and that moment of pausing can make all the difference in the world.

Law #5 The Law Of Relentlessness

The law of relentlessness emphasizes the need to keep going. To not back down when setbacks occur, to see them as feedback, and to stay on the path you intuitively believe is the path to freedom. Many people don't believe they have within them the ability to be relentless. But once I remind them of how relentless they were in pursuit of their current wife or husband, how they built their business from scratch, or how hard they worked to save up for that vacation to Rome, they begin believing something else. We all have this within us; we're just scared to use it for the anxiety-healing journey. We're scared that if we are relentless and fail, we may run into lost time, much effort that went unrewarded, or we might actually overcome anxiety (seriously, this is a fear for so many since anxiety = safety). My response to this is, please stop talking yourself out of your healing. The only thing holding you back is you and the excuses you have in response to full healing from anxiety.

Relentlessness doesn't mean fighting, though, it means applying with trust and faith. Consistently apply what you know in your heart will work, have trust in your ability to heal, and build your faith in the uncertainty that is to come. Edmond Mbiaka said it best when he said, "Every beautiful thing that life has to offer, demands the habit of relentlessness." How true.

Law #6 – The Law Of Transition

The law of transition emphasizes that you must turn from being a student to being a teacher toward yourself and for others. Gaining knowledge and the tools is great, but at some point, you must direct yourself toward the application of that knowledge and those skills. Also, people often ask me how to overcome the last hump, the 15% they have left to go over their anxiety. I regularly tell them that they must begin moving that advice from their minds to the minds of others. They must share their knowledge and look for every opportunity to do so. I can't tell you how many times a client provided a small snippet of advice to a friend in need only to feel tremendous self-confidence in themselves and the new belief. You must see yourself as willing to open your mind up to all possibilities, and capable of all future results. No longer are you someone who watches, listens, or reads about anxiety recovery and believes they've done enough to heal only to find themselves getting even more anxious. Continue to teach yourself and others, lending a compassionate approach to the healing journey. Respect the transition, love the transition, and get ready to leave the "coper," the manager, the hoper, and the wisher behind for good.

Law #7 – The Law Of Anticipation

Anticipate future challenges, and you'll be prepared to roll over them. Expect a day without any hardships whatsoever, and you'll be disappointed, as well as begin labeling yourself negatively and wrongly again. This law emphasizes the need to prepare for the future, not in an unhealthy and frantic way as anxiety sufferers usually do, but in a way that emphasizes the right mindset and skills should the challenge arise. For example, let's say you're invited to a party. The moment you hear about the invitation, you get those "icky" feelings in your stomach (or elsewhere). The immediate response is to cancel because your anxiety most likely won't allow you to have a good time, and you may say or do something stupid. That initial response is normal; you're still sensitized. Another option is to go and play it safe, hanging out in the corner, leaving early, or even bringing a support person with you. The final and most empowering option is to anticipate the specific challenges that may arise prior to, during, and after the event. Prior to the event, you feel you may rush to get ready, therefore causing you further pent up pressure within. As you anticipate this challenge, you can consciously begin slowing your speed, thus sending more safety signals throughout your nervous system. During the event, you may anticipate a large crowd of people, and large crowds make you more anxious. As you respond to this limiting idea, you realize that it's an opportunity to build your social circle of friends and a great opportunity to speak up. At the end of the event, you anticipate being physically exhausted by the whole thing, as you quickly remind yourself that it's good exhaustion since you strengthened your conscious thinking and reactions, and lessened the power of your unconscious anxious habits.

The key is to be specific. Don't just say it's an event, or it's the drive, or it's my workout that I'm anxious about. Instead, ask yourself what it is about those things that you are anxious about and anticipate them prior to responding differently. The law of anticipation has been instrumental in my healing as it helped me to differentiate what I truly had control over (aspects of my inner world), and what I had no control over (the results and other people). Many moments of clarity, which must be placed in your clarity journal, can come from applying this law regularly. Since the anticipation, preparation, and new response will create a new result.

Law #8 – The Law Of Alignment

Everything has a frequency and vibration and attracts to itself what is in harmony with itself (in the case of humans, it's the subconscious programs/core beliefs). Everything we see and experience in the physical world has its origins in the invisible, mental world. Your mind is a part of the universal mind, the infinite intelligence that lies in what cannot be seen but can be felt. Your emotional states, as well as your external results, will show you what you are in alignment with. To give you an example of this, think about commercial airplanes. Why is it that their cruising altitude is 35,000 to 40,000 feet? Because there's less friction at higher altitudes, and it's fuel-efficient, allowing the airplane to travel farther. If the airplane flies higher, the oxygen becomes too sparse to fuel the engines, and if the plane flies too low, the air resistance is greater. When a human is in a flow state, a place of effortless manifestation of everything good, they are cruising at just the right altitude. Their perceptions are flexible and consistently move toward considering the whole picture. Their words are controlled and empowering, and their behaviors are beneficial to their personal progress as well as to others.

Take a few minutes to recognize what you're currently aligned with. Is it love or fear? Acceptance or hate? Are you currently in a flow state, or are you fighting for everything? When we can become relentless and leave the results to the timeline set by the outer creative intelligence (God, if you prefer), we will then experience this life the way it was meant to be experienced. Fun will come back into our lives, and our childhood playfulness will show up again and again.

Summary:

- Clarity is key, and we must spend an extended amount of time building on our newfound clarity as it arrives throughout the day. The best way to do this is to carry a clarity journal and input your new realizations when they happen.

- Anticipating a challenge prepares a person to adopt the proper mindset, and bring their responding tools with them in their toolbox for healing (in future chapters). This goes a separate direction from avoiding the situation or doing what you can to fight or cope with the situation. Preparation is essential.

- The power of providing advice that you are adopting by your teachers is essential to healing. Take yourself out of the student role and into the teacher's role to overcome the last 15% or so of your leftover emotional distress.

- Optimism must be strengthened daily by becoming open to the possibilities of other future outcomes. Self-doubt will begin to fade as optimism grows.

- Relentlessness is a personal trait that already lives in the majority of people. Transferring this human quality from one aspect of life to the healing journey over anxiety is an essential component of long-term change.

CHAPTER 7:

The 4 Subconscious Programs That Are Crushing Your Spirit

"You're not used to being healthy, so you have no idea how to handle it when it arrives."

The subconscious mind-body (body because any part of the body can store an icon of memory) has an amazing capacity to store unlimited information. It is the most loyal servant as it does everything it's programmed to, and has the most up-to-date information (sensing the future and warning you in different ways). It is a goal-seeking mechanism, and if it has no consistent direction given to it, it will float around aimlessly. All our behavioral problems, psychosomatic illnesses, and personality disorders have their roots within the subconscious mind. One of the most important jobs of the subconscious mind is to regulate and control the mechanisms of the emotional and physical body. Efficiency is the goal of your entire nervous system — the less conscious interference, the better (from this deeper side of you).

While in the womb, there's no difference between the child and the mother. Most depressed mothers bring to the world depressed children since a mother's most consistent emotional state during those first 9 months is transferred directly to the child. Many times during my sessions, I'll regress a client back to the first scene/situation that has everything to do with their anxiety today. And just like that, they're back in the womb (more commonly they're within the ages of 0-7). The conscious mind has no access to this information until the person is in more of an altered hypnotic state, which is when the missing pieces of information relating to their anxiety show up. Taking care of their present distress at the root is 100 times more effective than giving someone coping techniques to just get through a current sensitizing situation. It's like cutting your grass, would you rather cut the top ends and leave it as it is? Or would you cut the grass at the roots so that it looks clean and maintained? The answer is at the root, of course, so f**k coping and start healing.

The earlier we go in a person's childhood, the more profound the effect it will have on the adult. This doesn't mean conversing about it as is common in psychoanalysis, that's like throwing a Hail Mary and hoping some result shows up just by circling the root cause, it rarely works, and when that "aha" moment shows up it could be years down the road. Instead, reframing past emotional traumas (as we'll touch on later in the book) can cure any current mental, emotional, and even physical issues a person is dealing with. This is what my experience working with thousands of people worldwide has taught me. It's also important to note that when reframing past experiences, we mustn't get caught up in whether we're working with the root cause or not. Instead, we should trust that whatever comes up will be beneficial to us. As we get deeper into strengthening the skill of reframing, we'll continue to open ourselves up to other experiences from our past. Depth is our goal; it's the key to true and lasting freedom. But not enough people are willing to explore their current distress in depth. You're different, though. You're determined, relentless, and will do whatever it takes. Because the opposite possibility of healing fully would be much more painful to live with long-term.

Getting into an altered state simply means to relax the mind and body at a level where you feel you're truly "letting go." People think hypnosis is giving up total control over their conscious mind and body; this is untrue. Anxiety sufferers, though, have connected relaxing to something negative. To them, it may be selfish, unproductive, dangerous (in case an external danger presents itself), or some other reason connected to their upbringing. Aristotle said it perfectly when he said, "Give me a child until he is 7 and I will show you the man." The four subconscious programs that are tucked away deep within you can all be attributed to what you saw, felt, heard, and so forth between this time period. This is because the greater the influence, status, or authority of the person providing the suggestion at this time in your life, the more readily accepted the idea is within the subconscious mind. This doesn't change as an adult; you're still more likely to take in the suggestions of your authority figures today unless you do some conscious intervention around the suggestion after it's given. Unfortunately, awareness and consciousness are rare in today's world. It's a skill that has never been truly developed by many people, including myself, growing up. People think that they're thinking about a situation when, in reality, they're just reliving their previous responses. And so the unconscious behavior follows, the same emotions are felt each day, and not a whole lot of real change occurs in a person's inner or outer world. Through this book, you will gain the understanding and proper mindset, as well as the skills and awareness, to heal your anxiety for good. So, let's get into the four subconscious programs that are currently leading your life down the wrong path:

The Inferiority Program

This program relates to the ideas of not being good enough, not having enough, never amounting to anything, and beliefs such as I'll always be inferior to the world. The millionaire motivational gurus today know very well that you have this running within your subconscious and provide you temporary jolts of dopamine and serotonin (your motivation and feel-good molecules) so they can sell you something. That something is rarely targeted at the root of your distress; it's too general an answer to be effective, it rarely comes with any personal support, and it's simply an opportunity to upsell you on the next motivational product. Smart little bastards, aren't they? People who carry this program within them realize that it never seems to go away on its own, and they are at the mercy of one idea. A single idea that floats into their minds could easily and swiftly lead them down the road toward inner chaos and outer drama. The next thing you know, they're in a situation that could easily have been avoided had they questioned the limiting idea (known as

Responding within the RIC framework). But to question the limiting idea goes against the subconscious program, and most likely will come with tremendous rejection. Remember, the subconscious mind is a goal-achieving agency; whatever was put there at the earliest days of your life must be fulfilled no matter what. This mind doesn't know the difference between good or bad for you; it just knows what came first and what was repeated most often. To question the limiting idea without emotion, without dissatisfaction, without further facts on why this limiting idea is utterly false and in the past, and without action, will leave the person running the same patterns of emotion and behavior. This is the difference between reacting, which is unconscious, and responding, which is conscious until it becomes positively unconscious.

When a person can emotionally reframe what is referred to in the Course of Miracles as the "moment of separation" (the initial sensitizing event) that cemented the program in the first place, as well as consistently respond to the idea and feeling that they get in the moment, reality shifts. These two components — reframing and responding — are the very spines of this book, the keys to freedom for you, and the people who rely on you. At this point, you might be wondering, "What if I'm in the reframing process with a practitioner who specializes in reframing, and I reframe an experience, and it's not the initial sensitizing event?" This question is due to the strong need for an anxiety sufferer to gain total control over the situation again. To that, I say, trust, have a little faith for goodness sake, and start enjoying the process rather than looking to make sure every dot is connected. Trust your intuition at that moment, that whatever comes up as far the age, the location, the people involved, etc., is the truth.

Reframing is a daily practice, and responding is a moment-to-moment practice. To eliminate the inferiority program, we must prove to the subconscious mind that the opposing — more rational and helpful — perception is safe to adopt. For safety to be projected, we must be relentless in our reframing and responding processes. Because if you think about it, you should be quite proud of the fact that you have anxiety. I mean, you mastered it and can go into it at a moment's notice! That's a skill that's been built up throughout the years. And the truth is if you can make anxiety and inferiority so automatic, you can also make inner peace, unconditional personal love, and empowerment automatic as well.

The Self-Punishment Program

"I must suffer, mentally, emotionally, or physically through life because suffering is part of who I am." Does this sound familiar? No wonder inner peace becomes such a challenge to experience for people with this program. The self-punishment program is taught. As a child, you saw your parents with a lack mindset, struggling to get by, and consistently wincing in discomfort and physical pain. You also began associating progress to self-punishment. If there was an area of your life that you wanted to improve, you had to go through tremendous internal pain and distress to achieve it; at least that was the idea. Here is where we clearly meet the incongruence between the conscious and the subconscious mind. The conscious mind says pain and struggle aren't necessary; in fact, it prevents progress. While the subconscious mind has a deeply embedded program that it believes is the truth and must be fulfilled no matter what. This is referred to as the calling. It's like an athletic coach with one goal for his team: win! The subconscious mind's programs are the objectives that need to get met, and the calling is the coach who will do what he can to fulfill these goals no matter what. Since 95% of what we think, feel, and do throughout the day is based on our subconscious programs, the 5% conscious mind has very little say. And during those times when we are conscious, it's pretty half-hearted. An idea that would be nice to adopt becomes short-lived because there's been no momentum in the build-up of that idea in the past.

The happiest, most at peace, and successful people don't suffer to meet their goals. Instead, they have created systems that they follow each day and trust that the result they would like will show up. The keyword here is trust. Habits reprogram the subconscious mind and relay the message that suffering goes against its main intention for us, our physical survival.

Continued harboring of self-punishment is the main reason people experience a series of recurring "accidents" in their lives or near-death experiences. You may believe that external things that happen to you are just accidental, when in fact, it has everything to do with these four programs. This is because the heart is the most powerful generator of electromagnetic energy in the human body. When this energy is emitted, it holds information encoded within it that can be detected many feet away from the human body. This is why when you walk by someone, you get a sense of what his or her emotional state is like.

Studies performed at HeartMath institute reveal that a person's heart signal can deeply affect another person's brainwaves and that the heart-brain synchronization can occur between two people when they interact. In the anxiety world, this means that the subconscious programs you're running like a record on an endless loop become what you consistently feel and what you think. What you feel and what you think will affect the results you get in your life, because they will affect your perceptions and behaviors.

An important message I give to my anxiety warriors on my Facebook page is "question everything." Instead of accepting the belief that life is and always will be this way, and I am, and I will always be this way, why not begin questioning everything instead? The biggest obstacle to questioning your core beliefs and your current identity comes in the form of your parents. Since questioning yourself essentially means question them, and questioning them would mean disobeying them, and boy, did you ever get an earful or even a smack if that was the case. You can see now why we unconsciously associate pain to change. Many times we don't know why we cycle in and out of clarity, inner peace, and good feelings only to finally realize that it has everything to do with our deeply embedded connections to our authority figures and caregivers. Questioning everything doesn't mean being disobedient. Wouldn't your parents want you to improve yourself? Wouldn't they deep down be proud of you as you excel in different aspects of your life? Of course they would, even though they may not have shown this kind of support to you on the outside. So question everything about yourself and keep questioning everything until seemingly out of the blue more aha moments show up! Every a-ha moment leads to greater insight into the need to let go of self-punishment. It serves no purpose, it's not safe, it's not noble or a moral obligation, it just prevents you from reaching your inner goals.

Fear Of Responsibility Program

The idea that life is easier when someone has very few responsibilities keeps a person fearful of ever committing to anything. Avoidance behaviors creep in quickly, and the person associates safety with living small. Anxiety becomes heightened just by thinking of stepping out of a person's comfort zone. To physically be in it, feels like a brush with death. This is a debilitating subconscious program because it strengthens the narrow mindedness of the individual, and weakens their ability to broaden their perceptions and see the big picture.

Not only does the fear of responsibility and these other programs lead to avoidance behaviors, but it also paves the way for:

- Escape strategies – Planning escape routes in case the feelings in the body get too overwhelming.
- Safety activities – Consistently relying on someone or something to curb or soothe their anxiety.
- Sensitization – Obsessing over how to cope with events leading to constant worry, leading to emotional and physical depletion.
- Eating or drinking disorders – Distractions to provide comfort away from the realities of anxiety. This can be food, alcohol, drugs, etc.

Sound familiar? Release the guilt and replace it with acceptance. These are natural tendencies that direct us based on our survival instincts. You've been a victim of an inner mechanism that began attaching threats to things that aren't, but you've rationalized that they are so many times over and over again in your head that your body started believing the story. It's like when you were a kid and mommy or daddy was telling you a bedtime story. Your imagination would take over, and your emotions would become heightened; you were so intrigued over what would come next in the story. Was it real? No. It was just a story that was told the right way that you made into pictures in your head. Your imagination took over, just like it unconsciously does today with anxiety as you continue to believe a catastrophic story instead, become emotional by it through the pictures in your head, and then act on it.

Let's be honest; this is no way to live a potentially beautiful life.

The fear of responsibility is a manifestation of past desires and actions that led to disappointing outcomes again and again. Expectations weren't met, so you learned that if you ever commit to something or try to create something on your own, you'll fail, so best to leave it to others. This program prevents people from healing from anxiety faster than they potentially can because a part of them believes that they'll never be able to follow through with what they commit to, so they look for the magic wand or the magic pill instead. This is when you hear the words, "I've tried everything." They tried everything and committed to nothing, and they don't realize it. But the subconscious programs are doing their job of protecting the person from committing (in case you get disappointed again and feel the same level of negative emotion and disappointment you did before).

I had this program running for decades. It began when I was 5 years old (my initial sensitizing event) and I was building my Legos. My dad walked in and quickly took over, putting my Lego blocks together, step by step, and not realizing that I was looking forward to doing it myself! I think he felt that I was taking too long and that I just wanted the Lego set to be finished so I could play with it. But he didn't realize that the part I enjoyed the most was the creation process, not the end. I was crushed, and since I didn't get too many Legos to build because we were so poor, I came to an understanding that if I didn't do things quickly, I shouldn't do them at all. And since nothing worth achieving is done quickly but over time instead, I found myself not committing to anything worthwhile. One childhood experience, such as this, has the potential to create millions of self-destructive connections in the brain. These connections are the very things that form the personality of a person and the GPS to cautiously navigate the world.

The above is an example of why conscious parenting is so crucial. Too many parents today don't realize how much of a loaded gun they are walking around with. Everything they think, say, and do becomes the programming within the child. When the child turns 5 years old, a part of their subconscious mind, called the critical factor, shows up. This is like the bouncer at a nightclub. As the bouncer sizes up the person who wants to get into the club, he checks his attire, his attitude, his character, and if it all fits, he's allowed to enter. If the person doesn't match the vibe of the club, he's rejected and sent away.

Think of your critical factor as that bouncer, and your subconscious mind as the club, and the people in line as your thoughts. If the thoughts don't align with your subconscious programs, they are immediately rejected, but if there's a match, they are accepted in, only to strengthen the original programs. What altered state work, and more specifically, hypnosis does, is it sends that bouncer (critical factor) out to lunch temporarily, giving direct access to communicate with the subconscious mind. This is why the power of reframing memories can make such an impact on a person's overall health.

Stephen Parkhill, the author of the book "Answer Cancer," was known for having a tremendously high success rate in curing cancer. People would come to him with only weeks to live, and as he regressed them to the cause, he helped them discharge their repressed emotion and get forgiveness, which led many times to a physical cure. How he never made the mainstream is beyond me; he was a miracle worker, and his teachings must continue to survive so that we can all get a deeper understanding of the mind-body connection.

The health of your cells depends on the state of your emotions.

This is to wake you up and to say start recognizing the components that lead to how you feel. You are not inferior, your parents felt inferior, and you just became a replica of them and their belief systems. You are a limitless being who has come to this world to share your uniqueness, not to fit a mold like the rest of the sheep out there. One of the most powerful emotions that I needed to summon to see past my inferiority program was anger.

We all walk around with a certain amount of repressed rage anyway. So I thought, why not use this toward becoming dissatisfied enough with being inferior so that it would force me into doing things differently. Anger was my driving force. I can't tell you how many times after that realization that I reframed that Lego experience in my imagination, telling dad exactly what I wish I could have during my initial sensitizing event.

At first, I located where in my body I was holding the inner rage still (my stomach), I then recognized what color was attached to that feeling (black) since color is an infinite language that the nervous system understands. I then added a few more elements, which we'll discuss more in the reframing chapter to get to know this distress even better. To not run from it or stuff it aside anymore but to look right at it and say, "You don't belong in this body anymore!" I proceeded in my mind's eye to shout at dad, telling him, "I WANTED TO FINISH THAT LEGO!" That was MY moment, and he stole it from me. I proceeded to knock down his completed version with my feet, and I ordered him to leave my room (brave young 5-year-old, I know) as I slowly went through the creation of that Lego set. As I finished it, I felt a sense of deep satisfaction; I physiologically felt a change in my adult body as I was reliving this through my mind's eye. I proceeded to show everyone what I had done with great pride and forgave my dad with a long lasting hug. I'll never forget the feelings I got from that hug. I made peace, I had restored my dignity as a 5-year-old, and I didn't feel like a mistake anymore. That hug was magical, and it always is when I walk my clients through their reframing exercises as they discharge their emotions, as well as receive or provide forgiveness.

As the experience came to a close, I paused the moment I felt the safest in my mind movie so that anytime I was reminded of that experience, I saw it in a way that helped me rather than harmed me. I never wanted that paused moment to end. It was total freedom.

I was angry with my dad; I had to be to get the point across and to discharge what I had been carrying around from that event that led to strengthening my inferiority program. We can use our emotions to fuel our healing and drive us forward, or we can repress them and release them onto others who don't deserve it. The choice is always ours.

The Perfectionism Program

This one's far too prevalent today in the anxiety world and is consistently connected to OCD. It says, "I must do things perfectly to fulfill the need for love, acceptance, connection, and significance that wasn't fulfilled when I was a child." We take on each day as two people; the first one is our adult self, and the second one is our inner wounded child self. The inner wounded child shows up through our thoughts, emotions, imagination, and our unconscious actions. The adult self is just fulfilling the rules of reality that were set by the younger self. We become a slave to perfectionism because it's the only chance we have to please our parents and authority figures, and be less ridiculed and feel like our presence in the world wasn't a mistake after all. Nothing we ever did was good enough for our authority figures. We never ate enough vegetables, we never trained hard enough, we never had enough friends, we never got good enough grades, we never smiled enough, we were never creative enough, and we were never good enough. Make no mistake, though; we can't blame our parents and past authority figures for this and the other programs. Just ask yourself, where did they get their information and education from? And what were they dealing with at the time?

This perspective is called placing yourself in second and third position. Second position is to see a frame (an experience) from the opposing person's perspective. Third position is to see the experience from an outsider's perspective (or a security camera's point of view, for example). Blame and guilt are poison, and we carry these emotions with us in our mind and bodies until we can begin seeing past experiences from other angles, and begin taking valuable lessons from them. I can't tell you how quickly perfectionism has the potential to end once we reframe a past situation and extract the lessons from it. That doesn't mean that one reframe will take away everything. It might, however, the power behind reframing is within the process combined with the relentlessness to keep reframing the same experience until it no longer has a negative emotional stranglehold on you. Once that experience has been neutralized, you would again place yourself into a calm state, trust what comes up, and proceed to reframe the next past experience.

Perfectionism isn't a problem until someone believes it's a problem.

Someone might believe that it's just who they are, and the last thing anyone wants to alter is who they think they are, that is until enough pain arises. What we are not told about perfectionism is that there's a big difference between working to be perfect and striving for personal progress. Perfectionism is about meeting our goals in order to impress or please others. Striving for personal progress, on the other hand, is about achieving your goals in order to be pleased with yourself, and to better your self-worth and self-concept. Striving for personal progress is internally motivated, whereas perfectionism is externally motivated. Where do you currently live? The other huge problem with perfectionism is that a person's self-worth is dependent on their ability to achieve their unrealistic goals. Your self-worth is dependent on the personal progress you're making through life, not by the rules that were set in stone early on. If you're currently going through the transition away from your perfectionism program, you must:

- Learn how to be vulnerable and have faith in the uncertainty that will come.
- Stop comparing yourself to others, and begin focusing on personal progress.
- Evaluate your perfectionism logically.

From one recovered perfectionist to a future recovered perfectionist, you have many currently hidden talents and qualities about you that will soon come out. See past your perfectionism tendencies when they show up, as you defy your unconscious actions one moment at a time. Soon, life will begin opening its arms to you and inviting you into more and more opportunities for self-growth and contribution.

Summary:

- These subconscious programs will consistently override your conscious desires if the conscious desires are too general, without emotion, and without a clear vision.

- All four of these programs are almost entirely connected to childhood experiences. There is, of course, a viable debate over how much of them are genetic, as well as the impact of generational trauma. Can toxicity also play a part? Absolutely. The funny thing to keep in mind, though, is that when a person begins seeing a shift in their mental and emotional state, they also gravitate away from toxic environments, people, and food. They even start losing their excess weight, since too many people today are dieting the physical body only to be met with disappointment, when in fact they need to diet the emotional body instead.

- Reframing memories, and responding effectively in the moment of anxiousness are the keys to personal progress. We will be touching on these 2 vital aspects of healing later on in the book.

- You are not what you think or feel; many times, they're just best guesses.

- Your external reality and your perceptions shift completely when your subconscious programs are altered. Instead of looking to change your external reality and other people, look to change yourself instead.

CHAPTER 8:

Effective Goal Setting
for Healing Anxiety

*"You are the only one who loses by
harboring an unforgiving mind."*

Many anxiety sufferers never heal their inner distress because they don't know when they've gotten "there." There, being that point of inner freedom and self-love that begins to radiate healing energy throughout the body and into the atmosphere. This may be just as important as any skills and techniques we discuss in this book because if you don't have a clear signal for where you want to go, your inner GPS will take you toward the thoughts and emotions that have been the most familiar (chaos and suffering). We don't want that; we want you to move into someone new and keep the characteristics that go along with that new identity. Since we consistently have two voices in our head — one wanting to do something new and the other reminding you of all the bad that could come from doing it — a specific and measurable plan toward healing anxiety can bypass this critical voice.

Similar to a crew on a ship with a captain giving orders (conscious mind) and sailors guiding the ship (subconscious mind), without orders, the sailors would crash into the rocks.

The key with effective goal setting toward healing anxiety is to set goals around what you want, not what you think is achievable. The two main reasons why we don't reach our goals are because they are not specific enough, and we quickly lose sight of them. As we begin fulfilling our personal goals, we move from living in effect (feeling like the victim of our circumstances and life) to living in cause (understanding that we create our circumstances, taking responsibility). What is expected tends to be realized; this is the #1 rule of the mind, so let's begin understanding where your life is headed.

As we go through the five steps to proper goal setting for healing anxiety, make sure you write down each of these questions and study them so you can understand yourself better.

1) Who

Questions:

Who do I desire to become?

The worst answers to this are: "I want to be happy," or "I want to end anxiety." The subconscious doesn't understand these directions since happiness could literally mean rage since that's what was presented first as a child and the most repeatedly from your parents fighting and arguing over the littlest things. What your parents said and did are the definitions of love at an unconscious level for you, until you change the definition. "I want to end anxiety" is also not good enough because it's too broad, it's not based around sensory language, and there's no real emotion behind it. Here's how we truly get the message across to your subconscious mind. Each of these has an internal and an external component to them.

- What will I see when I am anxiety free?
- What will I hear?
- What will I feel?

Your senses are the raw building blocks to your thinking. The more specific you get in terms of what you want within sensory-based language, and the more often you remind yourself of these, the more emotion arises. And since emotions are a language that your subconscious understands, this is how we communicate with it that a change is taking place; a new direction is on the way. Here's an example of how I built up my "who" responses when I was setting my personal goals:

- I will see myself as capable of achieving anything I consistently direct my focus toward (internally seeing). I will see what's right in others (externally) rather than what's wrong with them. I will see past criticism and take the lessons, if there are any, toward bettering myself.

So what will you see when healing anxiety shows up? Write down as much as you can right now related to what you'll see internally (new perceptions) and what you'll see externally in the outside world.

105

- I will hear myself using powerful words (internal) like transition, progress, and healing, rather than words that promote a victim mindset. I will listen to sounds like the birds chirping in the morning (external hearing), and notice my breath during meditation. I will also deeply listen and clearly hear the words from other people during conversations.

What we hear dictates our self-image. Many times, anxiety sufferers are so internally focused, dreading the next life situation, that they are rarely conscious of the sounds coming from the outside. Write down what you will hear internally and externally when healing is met.

And finally, write down what you will feel:

- I will feel emotionally neutral and physically capable (internal), and I will feel the texture of the leaves in nature, the sand between my toes, and the wind on my face as I go about my day (external).

As you can see, the feeling aspect of who we want to become is very specific — internally through feelings, and externally in physical contact with things. Write down as much as you can for this part as well, which finishes off the "who" section of goal setting for healing anxiety.

2) What

What things have I put on the shelf during my anxiety that I will get back into when i've overcome anxiety?

Write down as much as you can around what you've put aside and have become physically and mentally incapable of doing due to your anxiety. A few examples I had written down during my days with an anxiety disorder were:

- I've put aside my love for all sports and stopped joining local competitions that I will begin getting back into.
- I've set aside my one great business idea that I wasn't capable of diving into because of my emotional state daily. I will begin brainstorming ways on making this idea real once again.
- I've avoided local meetups to get to know new people because I didn't think they'd want to be friends with someone as anxious as me. I will slowly begin placing myself back into these meetups again as I will expect less from myself, allow for mistakes to occur, and just do it.

Your list might be quite long, and that's OK. Because much of this doesn't arrive in our consciousness from day to day since anxiety sufferers are so caught up in avoiding the next catastrophic situation. This list will help to create more usable pain within you that will bring to light all you're missing out on. The dissatisfaction will grow, and your actions will begin changing.

3) Where

Where do I see the main aspects of my life going two years from now after anxiety is behind me once and for all?

This is where you write down how the core aspects of your life will change two years from now; these include:

Health – What will your mental, emotional, physical, and spiritual health look like?

Relationships – How will you be interacting with people and what types of people will be in your social circle (be specific)?

Financial freedom – How much money do you intend to make and save?

Contribution – How will you contribute toward other people's lives in a positive way?

Leisure – What will your free time look like?

Write down these aspects of your life and what they'll look like two years from now post-anxiety, and give yourself full permission to feel what it will be like. Remember, again; it's the emotions that come with the goals that draw you toward the attainment of them. You can also certainly add more aspects if you choose. The more, the better.

4) Why

What is my biggest WHY for doing this?

Here's a letter I wrote to myself just after a failed suicide attempt.

I found myself stuck between the will to live and the desire to end my pain as I parked my car near a bridge I was planning to jump off. At that moment, I could have gone either way. What pulled me from completing what I had intended to do was the thought of my son being left without a father and leading a similar life of suffering as mine had been. I'm crying, I'm thinking, and I'm realizing that the pain of jumping off that bridge would haunt my whole family for years, so I didn't. I'll give it one more day and see what tomorrow brings. I expect very little, but that's enough for me to keep going. My child is the reason why I get to write this letter right now. I don't know what I intend from writing this, although I know it helps to put my thoughts onto paper to make things clearer to me. At this moment, I'm drowning less and analyzing more, which is more than what I can say I've been doing for quite some time now. Life is funny; it seems to hate me most of the time, punish me for simply being alive, or is it trying to teach me something? If there is a God, why would he punish rather than help? It makes no sense, and neither does me writing this letter right now when I could have been 6 feet under right at this moment. Anyway, thank you, my son, for the light that you are; nothing else could have pulled me from executing my end today other than you. Daddy.

The power of "why" was the one thing that pulled me out of completing my suicide attempt that day, nothing else. If I hadn't recently had a child, I would be dead right now, and that is the truth.

So what's your biggest "why" for putting this current distress behind you? Write down your one biggest why, and build on it in a way that creates even more awareness within.

5) When

When do I want to feel like I'm more solid in the new me?

The "when" is vitally important. It sends the signal of change to your subconscious mind and keeps you accountable for what needs to be done daily to move you in that direction. In my experience working with many anxiety sufferers, their freedom after doing the inner work comes between 21 days and three months. And when I mean freedom, it's important to get more specific into what that really means. What it doesn't mean is waking up to a trumpet of angels by your bed, floating to work on a magic carpet, and loving everyone and everything that happens to you (although all of that seems pretty awesome to me). Freedom means the ability to stay aware of your responses to an idea in your head, the emotions in your body, and a physical symptom that may still arise. As well, freedom means taking the positive from what's going on in your outside world. For example:

Your car breaks down before heading to work, which means you could easily curse the world, you, and your car. But instead, you recognize the opportunity you've been given to take the bus instead. The opportunity to spark up a delightful conversation with someone as you step out of your comfort zone, save $8 on gas, or listen to that new audiobook you just bought. It's never the thing that happens to us that's the problem; it's how we make it out to be in our mind that's the problem.

110

Write down a reasonable date that you'd like to be free from anxiety now. Remember, this doesn't mean pressure to make it happen; it means accountability to do what you need to. Heck, you might reach the goal, and you might not; it doesn't really matter. What truly matters is progress, and that's the deciding factor between staying stuck in inner distress and freedom from irrational fear.

What I'd like you to do once you've completed your goal setting is to place it on a wall so you can remind yourself each day of the transition you're in. You don't want to put this piece of paper somewhere where you'll just accidentally run into it months down the road; you want to consistently look at it daily and ask yourself at the end of each day whether you took steps toward or away from your goals. If you took steps toward your goals, you were conscious throughout at least some parts of your day; if you took steps away from your goals, it most likely shows that you were engaged in unconscious reactions (which is fine after a set period of time of conscious actions). The easiest thing to do is to repeat. Repeating how you normally think, speak, act, and what you imagine is the quickest way to dig yourself a deeper ditch. But what we do is we take the road less traveled, the uncomfortable one, and slowly make it comfortable over time. This doesn't mean that healing can't happen quickly, it certainly can, and I can recall many times when a person has done one of my guided meditations on my YouTube channels or a reframing exercise with me and overnight altered who they were. But we don't want to rely on this, instead, we want to trust in the process of healing, and work toward our goals each day.

Another thing to become aware of on this journey is how the universe will place what seems like insurmountable obstacles in your way when you start to alter parts of yourself. You may start thinking, "Isn't life supposed to get easier as I heal?" You can consider this a good sign related to the healing of your anxiety and becoming a new identity because it places you in a position to rise to the challenges rather than run from them, stuff them aside, or deny them, as you used to do.

Life will be wonderful again, I promise. Trust in you and never lose sight of who you're becoming.

Summary:

- The more specific you are with your goals, the better.
- The more emotional you get when you think about your goal as already achieved, the better.
- Welcome challenges rather than internalizing them negatively or hoping they never show up in your life. They're going to arise during the healing process. The question is, are you ready? How do you perceive them? And what do you do differently at that moment?
- Have a big enough WHY. Your why should be a daily reminder and should hook you right back onto the road of a warrior, and away from the path of a victim.
- Build your trust in yourself.

CHAPTER 9:

The Reality Map

"In order to gain control over ourselves,
we must first give up control over the
things we have little control over."

As we embark on this journey toward healing anxiety instead of coping and managing, we begin understanding the full process through the reality map. This map consists of four parts that explain a person's emotional state and what they're going through. You'll find yourself in any one of these four parts at this moment, and the map will give you a much clearer idea of the path you're on. The RIC-based reality map consists of:

1. A negative emotional state, which we recognize as being more internally based.

2. An active emotional state, which places a person into a more externally focused place.

3. A lighter emotional state where you begin feeling the reality of this shift from negative to positive. Externally directed.

4. A flow state, where you experience most, if not all, of your day with inner peace and taking life as it comes. Internally directed.

When we recognize the emotional states that come with each of these steps, it's the most consistent feeling throughout the day. Depending on where you are right now in your life, one feeling will dominate the day. Let's find out more about each level of consciousness and where you are right now.

Reality Map Stage 1

Darkness (Internally focused)

Darkness within stage 1 of the reality map is a place of profound negativity and pessimism. At this level of consciousness, the world is all-wrong. The person feels very much like a mistake — not good enough — consistently getting angry over little things, and feeling like they have lost all control. This is where people with anxiety disorders live. In this very internally focused place, nothing is worth doing because they already know the negative result of their efforts anyway (a self-fulfilling prophecy).

Some people experience this stage for moments throughout their lives, and others live here every day. If a person lives here every day, helplessness dominates, which can lead to finding more and more things to irrationally fear and be angry about. This anger and fear aren't so much about what is actually happening at the moment; it's an accumulation of these emotions that have been repressed for many years. The person experiencing these emotions may think that it's the present situation that's causing them to feel so highly aroused, but it's not. And because the person has done such a steady job of running from and stuffing these emotions, they don't do anything about the roots of their anxiety. They may think that they're taking care of their anxiety by getting massages, doing breathing exercises, or working out, but these are only coping strategies that temporarily discharge some of the repressed emotions. If they used these tools with the mindset of helping to uncover the missing pieces of information related to the roots of their anxiety, it would be fine. These are tools, like many others, that don't take you out of stage 1 and darkness but help you to understand how you got here and what keeps you stuck. As you can see, your mindset is tremendously important in healing anxiety, and for me, it comes before learning the skillsets. When in darkness, a person's memories look worse, and their future is bleak. These people are stuck in survival mode, just trying to get through another day with the hope and wish of something changing. Their prayers lack the emotional energy necessary to create the feelings that will get them moving forward, and their efforts to change are halfhearted at best. I lived here for years. I found temporary pleasure in junk food, video games, alcohol, and other self-sabotaging habits. People in the darkness stage rely on these bursts of temporary joy and in terms of anxiety, spend too much time asking other anxiety sufferers what to do.

Asking other anxiety suffers what to do, is like the blind leading the blind

Reassurance-seeking, in the hope of some sympathetic responses, creates a sense of understanding and connection. But soon, the connection becomes addictive, and suffering becomes a way of meeting the need for significance.

The biggest thing people in the darkness stage lack is structure. If only they could create a set schedule for themselves as to what to do and when they must do it, as well as let the results take care of themselves without attaching too much to them, they would begin climbing out of this hole. To this, there may be a response along the lines of, "I don't know what to do." But in truth, they do know what to do but are too fearful of committing to it. In this age of information overload, no one has any reason to say they don't know what to do. It's all there for the taking. The real question is, are they ready to begin healing? Readiness for this stage means less about being motivated and more about being clear. Clear about why a person believes what they believe, do what they do, and doubts themselves and the world the way they currently are. Depth is essential, and you must explore unknown territory if you are to shift your emotional state into one that consistently brings you flexibility in thinking in all situations.

Someone in this negative state spends around 95% of the day in their heads, and only 5% of the day on what's actually taking place on the outside. During conversations with others, they're more in tune with the catastrophic voices in their heads than they are with what the person across them is saying. They find themselves looking for distractions to avoid their thoughts and feelings only to find even more inner frustration. We must recognize these characteristics related to being in darkness and begin moving out of this stage as quickly as possible.

Reality Map Stage 2

Activeness (Externally focused)

In the activeness stage, an anxiety sufferer finds themselves getting more and more fed up with labeling themselves as a sufferer. They want to live more, they want to be more, and they want to meet with new outcome-focused people. This is a very active place in terms of recognizing and replacing those environments that drain their willpower points and people who are holding them back. It is also the time to pinpoint the skillsets they need to adopt. Their mindset is helpful in this stage as they realize that any discomfort felt in the present is leftover from childhood. This realization that their need for love, guidance, and acceptance wasn't met in childhood leads to fear that the bad feelings will get worse as well as rage in response to the feeling of not being taught right from wrong. In the stage of activeness, anger is used very effectively. Instead of repressing anger, or taking it out on people who don't deserve it, they use it to look fear in the eyes, confronting the darkness and rising to their challenges. This is an excellent way of beginning to discharge rage prior to reframing the past and future, as well as responding to, rather than reacting to, life's challenges.

A person in this stage starts to feel more connected to the external world. They are beginning to strengthen their awareness around their five senses since, in the dark anxiety stage, things were on such a negative autopilot setting. They begin finding themselves respecting new, helpful ideas and spending more time building on them. In this stage, a person must become aware of when they're doing too much toward their healing. This can emotionally and physically deplete a person, and they may find themselves right back in stage one of the reality map again. Instead, take a step back and take a daily inventory of how much you've been exposing yourself, journaling, reading, listening to podcasts, and so on. Is it too much? In the long run, could it hurt you more than it could help you? Be honest with yourself.

I really enjoyed being in the activeness stage of the reality map and found just the right balance between doing and receiving. You never want to feel like your healing is being forced to be accepted by your subconscious, you want to continue to convince this deepest part of you daily until it has no other choice but to accept the new beliefs and identity. So fall in love with yourself all over again in this stage, give yourself tremendous credit for doing what so many others would never even think of doing — changing who they are. Soon you will find yourself looking into the mirror (within the truest time of the day, the first 15 minutes upon waking), saying, "I am a proud warrior, and I can't wait to live this day fully. Let's go!"

Reality Map Stage 3

Lightness (Externally focused)

Stage 3 brings with it a transition out of activeness and very much into a "doing" place of enjoying the fruits of your labor. Now that the relentless inner work has been done, it's time to allow yourself to gently fall into a sense of lightness and self-pride. The weight of the world feels like it's mostly off your shoulders, the voices in your head are much more neutral and pleasant, and you question your potential for living in inner peace much less. Don't think it's all rainbows and unicorns from here, though; it's certainly not. Although life starts to feel a whole lot lighter, there's a very good chance of falling back into darkness if you aren't still strengthening your awareness. What I mean by this is you may begin to believe that life no longer comes with any challenges, and so when something does show up, it feels so foreign to the person who's gotten to a much lighter place that we can misinterpret it completely. It may feel like a total setback. One that in the mind of a person in stage 3 means they're right back in the darkness stage again. In this still highly externally focused place of progress, any negative idea, criticism, canceled plane trip, icky feeling in the tummy, action that you regret, catastrophic picture in your head, etc., is to be seen as normal.

Remember, it's what you do that matters, not what happens to you

These are just more opportunities from the universe to strengthen who you deserve to be. With all that aside, though, people in the lightness stage are much more empathetic toward others and much more compassionate toward themselves. They find themselves in places and teachings that are brand new such as yoga classes, meditation classes, and listening to spiritual or other types of leaders. The new energy that's pouring through you is being communicated to the outer, infinite intelligence, and you are being guided. You find yourself pulling farther away from your parents' and family's religious beliefs and into your own religious and spiritual ones. This is a great sign that you must entertain and give yourself more credit for. You realize now at an even deeper level that you can still wholeheartedly love people from your past and present, while respectfully disagreeing with them on these and other views. Your breath moves from shallow to deep, your posture improves, and the aches and pains in your body begin to fade. You start to understand that growing old doesn't mean growing into disease, but growing younger in terms of openness and playfulness as well as health.

As you move from stage 3 into stage 4, you might begin to see death from a new viewpoint as well. It's no longer a grim reaper, or hell, or the devil that will meet you in the end, but a mystical and beautiful transition into a separate form of consciousness. As the body passes, the spirit lives on; energy never dies but, instead, gets transferred, and these ideas are leading you to trust in the cycle of life more. When this trust is built up, you respect the components of life much more as well. You no longer fear the future or regret your past; you embrace the beautiful uncertainty of what's to come and take the lessons from yesterday.

Take time for deep contemplation now before moving on. Do you recognize what stage you're currently in? Is there a major lesson you have taken from this chapter? Analyze this now.

Reality Map Stage 4

Revival (Internally focused)

The final stage is revival; a place many people dream of but can only get glimpses of from time to time. In the revival stage, a person's positivity is on autopilot. They've done a fantastic job of doing the inner work and redesigning their identity. People in this stage see themselves as lucky all the time; it's like whatever they touch turns to gold. I'm sure you know someone like this. The person you keep asking, "How do you do it?" or, "What's it like being you?" In this place of being one with life, a person finds inner peace in the loudest environments, the most obnoxious people, and the most challenging scenarios. Life's challenges don't end, they never do, but people who have solidified being in the revival stage handle them as they would good experiences that come their way. With a calm faith that the outcome, no matter what it is, is for the greater good. These people have mastered themselves on the inside and understand that only now can they make a lasting difference in other people's lives. We come to this world being told that we must give, give, give, help, help, help, well who's going to help us? If one can only help and give very little, what benefit is that to others? Suddenly because this has become ingrained as a core belief, this person starts feeling selfish whenever they want to do something for themselves.

By becoming more selfish, you are helping others; you must understand this

This is because the subconscious mind picks up on energy fields, and people make prejudgments of you way before their conscious mind knows it. By carrying yourself with a certain vibration and frequency, you are inspiring others at an energetic level. You say a lot more through your energy than you do through your words. But today, people associate loudness with being courageous and strong while quietness is looked at as being weak and fragile.

People in the revival stage know better, and don't get caught up in these or other false impressions of others.

The important thing to note here is that you must go through all the stages to get to the revival stage. From a negative state to an active and doing state to a lighter and clearer state to a deeply connected and flow state. This is the only way to reach long-term freedom.

Many people don't understand this, and they try to go directly from one internal place (darkness) to another (revival). This is why people are growing more and more frustrated in the world and are becoming more violent and aggressive. If there isn't a discharge of built-up energy, it must go somewhere; therefore, disease happens. The emotions get locked in for decades without a safe and proper outlet, and a person continues hiding from what they must face and utilizing distraction methods, only to be met with a physical issue. Then they become shocked when they're given the diagnosis and become frantic in their need to get better. It's much easier to prevent disease than to heal disease, although the opposite can also be true depending on many factors within a person.

You are on this planet to thrive, not to just survive

Remember that. Everything you ever wanted is already right in front of you, and people in the revival stage know this. They are consistently happy people, they know their purpose, like-minded people gravitate to them, they make money easily, and so forth. Everything is connected, and in revival, everything is connected in a free-flowing and positive way. Nothing can go wrong because the meaning of wrong has changed to just life. It just is, and if it just is, it means that the experience and the emotions will come and go. People in stage 4 find an inner love and acceptance for themselves that they've never felt before. Everything about them is good. There is no bad anymore; there is no hate, nor is there regret. This level of consciousness takes the word "living" to a whole new meaning. As living is no longer attached to what you do, how much money you have, or how sexy your partner is; living is how well you get along with life's curveballs. Revived people live minimally, since emotionally and energetically it makes sense. Emotionally, because one piece of clothing isn't any better than the next, and energetically, because the less time spent on truly meaningless things, the more time is available for ideas that will better you and change the world, leaving you with plenty of energy in reserve.

Summary:

- An effective approach to healing anxiety comes with understanding the necessary journey through all four stages of the reality map, eventually ending in total revival.

- Darkness is a place you might be in right now, but it doesn't have to be your future. As long as you are in an active/doing place, you will strengthen your awareness and begin proving safety over what your subconscious deems threatening.

- During the lightness stage, setbacks in thinking, information being received by others, speaking, doing or not doing, must be expected but not attached to. Challenges are a part of the road to revival; embrace them.

- Different is good. It may be threatening to others, but it's necessary for your evolution.

- In the end, revival is an internally focused flow state. The desire to be liked, or to do and say the "right" thing, doesn't exist anymore. Instead, trust is built within the person, and within the one universal mind, which is the infinite intelligence that surrounds us.

CHAPTER 10:

The Master Framework for Healing Anxiety

"The awakened one sees cause and effect, while the pessimist sees only suffering and turmoil."

I've written this book to give people who are suffering from anxiety a whole new way of looking at their healing journey. We must remind ourselves that we came to this world to live a pleasant and virtuous life and with the innate intent to contribute to other people's lives positively. To thrive in this way means to experience continuous progress in all areas of our lives, to have faith in what we can't control, and to do all we can to control what we have control over — ourselves. For many years I was chained to an anxiety-filled life feeling tremendous pressure from all walks of life along with the pressure to get better. Life got too serious, and I paid the price every moment of every day. That is until I took a more structured approach to my days. I began putting puzzle piece after puzzle piece together, relentlessly doing the inner work, and consistently listening to what the next need was within me that wasn't being met (or was in a negative manner). I recognized a framework where I could implement the skills I had been learning. I loved the progress and the challenges as the days went on. If you're not enjoying the process of becoming a greater version of you, you'll revert to your old habits out of sheer frustration. I began asking myself questions like, "What's fun about this?" rather than, "Why does God hate me so much?" Ask a better question, and you'll get a better answer. The answers to "what's fun about this?" started showing up more and more, whether I was making a sandwich, taking a shower, or driving to work. What's fun about this led me to see things that I would have never been able to see had I let my unconsciousness take over.

The better you know yourself and your anxiety, the better chance you'll have for a swift healing journey. Understanding the conscious and subconscious factors that create anxiety takes a detective-like approach to healing. But this is only the beginning; there's much more to uncover and learn from as you take something new from each challenge you overcome.

It's time to create an overview of what the structure for your healing will look like. As we focus on these three timelines of change work, we are in the process of redesigning your new identity.

Past

The past, for most (if not all) anxiety sufferers, is filled with guilt over certain rules about life that were given to them when they were children. Those "broken" rules also created shame, because they feel they knew better, as well as remorse due to the consequences it led to. Regret puts the final touches on a helpless and desperate childhood due to feeling bad about the consequences to ourselves, having broken the rules of life. But here's an example of how someone can be led into a subconscious program of inferiority, as well as the fear of responsibility, that was created by no mistake of their own:

A mother and child are playing; the mother interacts with the child making the sounds that bring a smile to a child's face "goooo kooo goo!" The child responds pleasantly and feels an even deeper connection to his or her first god of their universe. Now the child initiates interaction, and the mother doesn't respond; the mother, for whatever reason, turns a blind eye knowingly or unknowingly. This child quickly learns that there's no reward gained by initiating communication, period. Since mom doesn't respond, why would anyone else? This becomes law within a person, and soon, avoidance behaviors and a lowered self-image become a big piece of their identity.

The mother or father doesn't realize what is happening because most likely, it's out of their awareness. The child grows up, becomes an adult, and believes nothing he or she ever does will hold any value toward themselves, others, and the world because the value is in the response. Since there was little-to-no response during the earliest years when the brain was beginning to make these powerful neural connections for future recall, the adult self says this is my reality. A diagnosed anxiety disorder isn't too far behind someone like this. Learned helplessness is developed, and anxiety and depression begin taking turns showing up in the adult's life as they are physically in the present, but mentally and emotionally still in the past.

The question is, what can we do about it? Well, within the RIC framework, one of the key components to long-term change work comes down to emotional reframing of these kinds of past events. As a person spends more and more time prioritizing themselves and spending time in meditation and nature, more of what needs to become reframed shows up. This is due to a feeling. The feeling itself is connected to a need that wasn't met no matter how hard we tried, and yet we're still trying with very little to show for our efforts. Within this framework, it's important to ...

Clean up our past if we want to fully live in the present

Here are the keys to doing this:

- First, recognize that denying or running from your past won't make it go away. We must courageously and safely dive into our past with the intention of renegotiating the situations that led to the freeze reaction.
- We must spend 5 to 10 minutes daily (longer, if needed) on what we believe is the experience or person that keeps holding us back today.
- We must commit to following through by verbally or possibly behaviorally fighting back or walking away from the situation because it was the freeze/helpless response that led to this experience affecting us in such a negative way today in the present.

As mentioned earlier, you must let your body do whatever it needs to do to discharge this stagnant energy. One person's lump in the throat may hold one highly intense and traumatic event that hasn't been reframed, or it might hold multiple events. No matter what the symptom, we don't deal with symptoms; we deal with causes. When a person's body begins shaking during or after the process, shake away. Crying? Cry like a baby. Yawning? Yawn it out. Respect the process the body must go through to reorganize the meanings of your past, and therefore open you up to a brighter future.

It's also important to understand the parts that hold a person back during this process of emotional reframing. Prejudgments prior to the process, not fully being absorbed during it, and not allowing full focus to be inserted into the process can ruin the chances of effective energetic discharge. Just make sure you have that talk with yourself prior to reframing your memories. Since I'll be guiding you through the process during the reframing chapter later in the book, you don't have to create the steps yourself. Remember, keep reframing the same experience or relationship to a person until you can look at it consciously and naturally and start seeing it from a new angle, as well as take away key lessons from it. The keyword is, naturally, which means not forcefully (in the hope of quicker progress). When you look at the experience from the past, and it creates a neutral emotion within, you can feel grateful that it happened because of the lessons you've learned. From this neutral position, you've forgiven anyone who needs to be forgiven, and you can give yourself time to dig deeper into the next feeling in your body connected to another experience. Trust what comes up during the process of cleaning up your past; don't overthink it. When you're mind and body are in a relaxed state, the critical factor (which protects the original subconscious programs) won't be present, leaving you in direct communication with your subconscious mind. It will speak to you in pictures, sounds, and feelings. Trust this communication. Go through the process daily until it's resolved, and move one more giant step toward truly letting go and becoming more than anxiety.

Present

Anxiety sufferers don't truly live in the present since unconsciously, they're still stuck in the past, and consciously, they're concerned about the problems that will take place in the future. As this book is a deep dive into the roots of your anxiety, we have to understand what fuels it in the present, which comes down to rage (not anger, most people are way past that) and a temper that discharges onto others when the opportunity presents itself.

Most anxiety sufferers feel a great deal of frustration because other people don't understand what they're going through. The sufferer feels like the rules of life are being broken because sympathy, proper advice, and empathy must be given at all times to them, and when it's not, more rage gets added to the original rage, and that's a lot of inner rage. This lack of understanding by others fills the heart and every cell in the body with hatred toward the world and themselves, and since the universe picks up on our feelings, your external results are no accident. Your path is laid out, and as much as you may not like it, it's what you've been communicating into your inner and outer world for quite some time.

Within the teachings of RIC, we don't fret over our inner challenges because we are outcome-focused people. RIC-focused individuals have a growth mindset, meaning they know they can grow out of their self-limits, and learn and apply new teachings to alter themselves fully. They don't get caught up within a lack mindset. A lack mindset promotes attitudes such as "life, and this struggle with anxiety, is too hard; none of it is changeable, and I must do my best to live with this forever." There are no victims here, only warriors who don't believe in fighting their inner selves, but understanding and compassionately guiding their inner wounded child to safety for the sake of their adult selves.

The keys to progress within present time are:

- Use your responding skills presented to you in chapter 20 to begin shifting the meaning of what's threatening to neutral.
- Strengthen your conscious mind's tremendous capability to think and organize external information better by staying aware, which is different from staying alert (the stress response).
- See your nervous system like Bluetooth, and understand that it automatically connects to and downloads the attributes of the people you spend the most time with. Take a good look at what information is being downloaded within, and make changes in the people and energy you surround yourself with now! Not tomorrow.
- Find a productive way to discharge the repressed rage in the present. Get back into exercising, take boxing classes, or start rock climbing. Whatever gets you moving, and preferably into nature more, will be a tremendous benefit to releasing

these repressed emotions along with cleaning up the past.

- Structure your sleep better. Get 7-9 hours of sleep nightly and go to bed before 10 p.m. (I know, what a downer I am) before your second wind hits around 11 p.m. for people suffering from adrenal fatigue. Your adrenal glands will quickly recuperate if you do this as well as disengage from stimulating activities before sleep. Also, be aware of blue-light activation, which lessens the amount of melatonin (sleep aid) you get. This blue light coming from your devices and TV turns on your cortisol, which creates a heightened state of awareness, the last thing we need during your healing journey.

We must understand that emotions are more complicated than we think. They are memories, decisions, values, beliefs, identity, survival, and ego all rolled up into a feeling that shows up. You're here not because you love the different toques I wear in my YouTube videos, or because of my calming voice on the Anxiety Guy podcasts, you're here because you want to change how you feel and make that change stick. The key in the present time during moments of being challenged is to create present state awareness before your thoughts and emotions take over. At the end of each day, people judge the day depending on whether they felt anxiety or not, when, in fact, they must review the day based on how well they responded to those situations. If you haven't already realized it, worry doesn't keep you safe from catastrophic events, or prevent physical illness, or help to control external events. Just thought I'd remind you in case you still believe it does.

Future

The question about why we feel stress, anxiety, and panic about the future comes with a very interesting answer. And that answer is because many don't feel like they have a set of stable rules set in place to follow, which then leads them back into present anger and increased temper.

Let's dig even deeper. The future is a battle between the conscious mind looking for structure and control in the inner world (which feels like it's getting more out of control by the day), and the subconscious that perceives chaos as familiar (because that's what was there when we were kids, and what has been repeated the most often). Which one wins? It's the 95% that runs the day — the subconscious mind, not the conscious mind, which is 5%. This battle is very evident in anxiety sufferers as you hear them utter the words, "I just don't know what to do or where to start." That's not really the problem. I mean, if you lived in the prehistoric days I could understand. But these days, all you have to do is input a few keywords into a search engine and whammo! It's like a genie appearing out of a lamp. The better question is, why does your subconscious mind prevent you from moving toward the answer, finding it, and committing to it until the desire is fulfilled? To understand this on a deeper level, rather than just the explanation of safety and familiarity that overtakes a person's actions and nonactions, we have to understand your reticular activating system.

We are experts at exaggeration (hence the anxiety) because the reticular activating system within each of us decides what you should become aware of from moment to moment. It decides this by what is of importance to you (based on years of habit) and what may be a threat to you. The reticular activating system is a mechanism that filters out information that isn't of value to you based on what your five senses take in. Its functions are:

Positive filtering – Like a mother, it's attuned to every sound her baby makes. The greater the positive emotion, the deeper the encoding for later recall to create the same good feelings.

Negative filtering – Filtering out the negatives that mean very little to you or is unhelpful.

Individual perception – To perceive things happening in a way that's different from others.

You can stop beating yourself up now for seeing the future in such a bleak way. It's not your conscious mind doing it; it's more so the parts of you that have been attuned to danger in the future. You believe with certainty that your future will be as disastrous as your past because your belief gives the appearance of being correct. The keyword is APPEARANCE; it gives the appearance of being correct, but it's not actually correct.

See it like a wild guess that gets strengthened each time you think and act in line with how you feel. You feel something bad happening in the future, and you start building on more and more ways it will go downhill, so more adrenaline gets secreted from your adrenal glands, and your conscious mind gets left out like a kid at a baseball game who got picked last. The next thing you know, you automate your thinking and acting based on how you feel.

You are literally a slave to your emotions at this point

In anticipating future challenges, we quickly estimate the significance of that challenge and match it up with the inner strength of our resources to respond to that challenge. The problem lies in the fact that we have no access to those positive resources if we continue seeing ourselves as incapable and undeserving of good. It's human nature to anticipate what's to come in the future. But with anxiety, we take it many steps forward, and it gets out of hand. The result is fear, apprehension, and eventually overwhelm.

From this day forward, do not allow anxiety to make you feel like you have to settle for less than what you truly want. Often, this leads a person to believe that good feelings are dependent on what happens outside of them, leaving them even more powerless in the process. I don't repeatedly say, "You are more than anxiety," in my YouTube videos and the Anxiety Guy podcasts because I think it makes me look cool; I say it because I want you to begin seeing through who you currently are. You are a manifestation of pure spirit, and pure spirit cannot live with anxiety as long as the heart believes this to be true.

Your future will either be as challenging as how most of your life has been until now or the complete opposite. Peace can overtake chaos, clarity can overtake the fog within the mind, and congruence within the mind, body, and spirit can overtake disconnection.

Here is what we must become aware of to make sure that the way we perceive the future is pleasant:

- Our focus on the future must turn from what could be missing to what could be possible. Where focus goes is where your emotions flow, so the more we take control of our focus — rather than allowing negative emotions to dictate our focus — the better.

- We must understand that we are the creators of our future, and it's not in the hands of anyone else. As we become emotionally aligned with optimism and what's good, what's good will consistently show up in every aspect of life. Remember, it's not what happens to you, but how you choose to perceive what happens to you that determines what your future looks like.

- We must stop restricting ourselves based on our age. Many people have grown up with the belief that as you grow older, the less you're capable of achieving and the worse you start feeling. FALSE! We all know that one (in my case, many more than one) person who completely defies this belief in every way. That is no accident; it comes down to understanding and habit.

- Stop entertaining the idea that your self-worth is determined by what you do for a living. This is the case if you live in North America, especially. Within the first 2 minutes of meeting someone new, the person asks, "What do you do for a living?" That question comes with a deep comparison from the person who asked the question. If he or she is in a more advanced position, they're a threat; if they make more money than you, they're a threat. They're already a threat because he or she is better looking, of course. You get the point.

- Use the word TRANSITION more when a bleak idea about your future shows up. When we replace words like always (I'll always suffer), failure (I'm such a failure), or suffer (I'll just suffer more in the future) with the word "transition," we can begin opening ourselves up to new avenues of optimism and positive change. Here's a quick test: right now, tell yourself, "I will always suffer," and then wait a moment. Notice how it makes you feel. Now tell yourself, "I am in a transition out of suffering," and then wait a few moments. Notice how that one feels. Substituting the word, transition, is a powerful way of responding to negative self-talk.

Summary:

- Anxiety sufferers are survivors — survivors of emotionally traumatic events that they're consciously or unconsciously aware of. The unconscious memories have been stuffed aside so many times that we've lost touch with these past experiences. Our present symptoms could very well be based on our past memories that have been re-accessed. If we continue reverting to distraction methods, like "turning up the music" in our car every time an "icky" feeling shows up in our body, or a past experience shows up in our mind, we're only compounding the problem. Instead of coping in this manner, depth, and a certain level of courage are needed. Reframing past memories through imaginative and somatic work allows us to renegotiate a new meaning over the past event, therefore changing the present trigger connected to the memory into something neutral.

- Understand that your past isn't a life sentence; it's a learning opportunity. And the more lessons you can take from those past experiences, the better it will serve you in any given situation in the present.

- Responding must overtake reacting in the present. Reacting means to think and act in line with your initial emotional response to a situation. Responding means to see an opposing perspective and to question the legitimacy of the anxious feelings that arise.

- Your future is yours to create. Enjoying the transformational journey from your old identity to the new one is an essential component to change work. If you're always reminding yourself how far you still have to go to get to where you want to go, you'll always be addicted to suffering. If you consistently give yourself credit for gently and compassionately guiding yourself toward freedom, you're well on your way.

- Your power words are an essential part of healing anxiety. Specifically, the words transition, progress, momentum, challenge (over trigger), guiding, and neutral (emotionally). Replacing your old vocabulary with a new, improved one is a part of the new you.

CHAPTER 11:

The Belief Scale

*"The biggest problem is that your
desires and beliefs don't match."*

Maturation is growing out of the mistaken beliefs about ourselves from childhood. Some people who are in their 80s still carry the same beliefs they had when they were 10 years old, and some people at the age of 15 have grown out of their beliefs from much younger. You are what you believe at a subconscious level. When dealing with anxiety, we're dealing with fatigue (even mental, emotional, or physical depletion), sensitization, and consistent catastrophic perceptions over future situations, inner conflict between our two minds, and identity-level issues (I am vs. I am doing). Each one of these is directly connected to our core beliefs. As these beliefs change through the inner work you do daily, so does everything else mentioned.

Through the works of Louise Hay and other related teachers, we can now directly identify the core beliefs and emotions a person holds within, that are connected to what they're experiencing in the physical body. Here are a few examples of this connection:

Back issues – Represents a perception over a lack of support in life, lack of emotional support, feeling helpless and hopeless (beliefs around learned helplessness)

Bladder problems – Holding onto old ideas, fear of letting go, being pissed off (beliefs around the pain of letting things go, and unforgiveness for themselves or others)

Cancer – Deep hurt, carrying hatred, longstanding resentment, grief

Dizziness – Scattered thinking, a refusal to see the opposing perspectives

Fatigue – Resistance to the flow of life, boredom, lack of love for what one does

Heart problems – Lack of joy, longstanding emotional repression, straining through life, stress and worry

Numbness – Withholding love and consideration, multiple highly intense traumas causing chemical protection and shock

Stomach – Holds in nourishment, dread, fear of the new, inability to assimilate the new

Lump in the throat and throat issues – No avenue of expression, inability to speak up for one's self, swallowed anger, stifled creativity, refusal to change

I've studied these, as well as many other symptoms, my clients come to me with, and the connection between repressed emotion and physical symptoms is incredibly consistent. Each one of these, along with many other physical issues, comes with core beliefs that become emotion, which affects a person's actions and ultimately creates a connection to identity. This is artificial living at its best — a result of years of conscious, subconscious, and subliminal programming that is now coming to the forefront. There are too many people in the world who wait until things get way out of hand within them, before doing something about it. Then they turn frantic in the hopes of quick change, which only amplifies the problem, and then attempt to make a 180-degree switch to a new identity with the help of a magic wand that doesn't exist. This was me. The closest thing to a magic wand that I've run into is reframing your memories. Other than that, you'll be left disappointed if you keep up with this desire to find a quick switch.

The Belief Scale:

The belief scale is a way to see where you currently stand in your subconscious beliefs vs. your conscious beliefs. By giving the belief scale some deep thought, many new realizations and epiphanies will come to you in time.

Level 1 Person – A level 1 person hasn't changed his beliefs over who he/she is, what they're capable of, what their external reality is like, and about other people. This person goes through life with the wrong kind of connections — negative connections between the core beliefs (subconscious) and conscious beliefs (ones we're aware of). When you are within the energy field of a level 1 person, you will most likely feel it unless you have little to no intuitive sense due to mental and emotional depletion. Level 1 people have not learned how to think through their problems, nor do they understand that they need to. They stuff problems aside every chance they get, rather than taking the time to teach themselves how to deal with challenges, usually due to a fear of commitment.

A level 1 person physically looks like they're aging with the same mental and emotional capabilities as when they were a child. This doesn't mean all hope is lost, however. With the right level of dissatisfaction and desperation, the mindset of moving toward discomfort rather than away, and with the right inner tools, anything is possible.

Level 2 Person – A level 2 person begins questioning his or her identity (who they are and what they deserve). They begin questioning their capabilities and what their higher purpose in life might be. They begin questioning the template (earliest experiences) of their reality that was provided to them by their authority figures. A level 2 person slowly begins to see a few situations from their past and present from other angles — mainly second position and third positions (the opposing person's angle, and an outsider's looking in). In this level of consciousness, there is curiosity brewing within, a curiosity that begins to open doors to what life can possibly be like. A person at this level spends a little more quality time by him or herself and begins analyzing more rather than unconsciously reacting. Remember, when curiosity (meaning a deeper look into the why's for what you're thinking and feeling) begins overtaking franticness during moments of anxiousness, you're well on your way to healing.

Level 3 Person – A level 3 person turns their questioning in level 2 into an awakening and begins tipping the scales toward believing different things. As the scales tip toward a change in personality, this person accepts the sacrifices that will have to be made to alter who they are, and what they believe, for good (these sacrifices are explained later in the book). This person begins to feel a shift in their reality happening; they begin understanding that the people in their past were doing the best they could (therefore, forgiveness begins showing up). The vision for their future, better version of themselves, becomes clearer and clearer. No longer are they feeling like a victim of their circumstances, but realize that what goes on within them results in what goes on outside of them.

Level 4 Person – This is when the transition in beliefs starts to get exciting. A level 4 person firmly believes that what he now believes is the real truth. It's no longer at a head level (an idea), it's now within a heart level (feeling), and gut-level (sensing). This person feels a sense of effortless communication within them, with others, and with the infinite intelligence we sense but can't see around our world (call it God). The level 4 person feels love and shares that love with others naturally, and fear is placed in its rightful spot.

Level 5 Person – A level 5 person trusts that everything that happens in life is for the greater good and is one with God, not separate. A level 5 person has connected him or herself to their superconscious mind — your higher self, or creative subconscious. This is the part of your subconscious that connects to the universe and creates miracles in your life (like spontaneous remissions, for example). At this level, there may even be a link between other dimensions and your physical existence.

The biggest difference between a level 1 person and a level 5 person is that the level 1 person has desires and core beliefs that don't match, whereas a level 5 person has fewer desires, more trust, and core beliefs that do match. I can confidently say that I've gone through all of these levels and have come out comfortably living as a level 5 person. My inner peace and contentment are as strong and automatic as my anxiety once was. But I could never have done it had I kept looking to go straight from level 1 to level 5 in my belief systems. This is a process that is backed by understanding the transmutation and gestation periods.

Transmutation is a universal law that says we take different forms as we go through the change process. In the anxiety world, that translates into saying anxiety will turn into depression, which will turn into mild stress, which will turn into social anxiety, which will eventually turn into your natural self through continued inner work. The principle of gestation teaches us that there's a timeframe that something must go through to become what it's meant to be. When we can understand these two principles of life, we can become patient and more compassionate with ourselves in the anxiety-healing journey, knowing that these are universal principles that must be applied until our desires are met. We can't choose when we'll become a level 5 person with beliefs that oppose the delusions we started this life with, but we can choose to prioritize ourselves and the inner work for the sake of ourselves and the benefit of this world.

Remember that altering a thought without altering the identity keeps you stuck in the same core beliefs you adopted in childhood. The "doing" during the change process isn't enough. It's the transition toward someone else that desensitizes you from all the things you're currently sensitized to. For many people who say they're ready for change, it's like putting your feet in a cold lake of water, only to stand there or scatter back to safety (old identity). The people who systematically or quickly thrust themselves into the cold water are led to the clarity needed to change their belief systems for good. Notice that it's only the initial few moments of getting into that water that it feels cold. Our perceptions change as our mental, emotional, and physical bodies adjust to the water. We begin feeling comfortable, and what happens most of the time? We don't want to get out! Eventually, when you do get out of the lake, you can't wait to go back and do it again. This is called a history of success. And the more moments of success such as this that you have where you walk the path you say you desire, the easier and easier it becomes to change what you believe. The subconscious mind will check its filing cabinet to see what occurred the last time this situation arose, and what will it find? That depends on what you do and how you handle the situation. But what we want it to find is a neutral or pleasant emotional experience so that the next time it can move you more easily into that same state during that experience.

The brain will keep doing what's familiar until there comes a time when we teach it something else

With this, we must also understand the importance of feeling good. The more you feel good, naturally, the faster you'll be able to rewrite your belief systems. You'll see this as a method many motivational speakers like Tony Robbins use today. Where he amps you up so that you feel like you're going to explode with positivity. He knows that these good feelings amplify neuroplasticity, and help to fire off neurotransmitters like dopamine (good feelings based around future rewards), serotonin (a mood stabilizer, creates the good feelings of social importance), and oxytocin (the bonding hormone, which creates the good feelings of trust). Because we are fully absorbed in the experience, we eat up his every word, and retain more, and leave the experience feeling euphoric. What we do with this momentum differs from one person to the next, but it's a good starting point so that you can get from level 1 all the way to level 5. It's all about knowing what you want and paying the price to get it. The price you have to pay are the habits you need to divorce yourself from, the connections you've made between worry and safety, and the false ideas and old core beliefs connected to your identity.

Your most dominant beliefs are holographic. That means that they're not just in your mind, body, and spirit, they're everywhere. And the beauty is that when you begin to level up and alter one belief, everything else will change. Rapid and permanent change happens when we integrate change work that focuses on the entire mind, body, spirit system. And this is where you see people go wrong, as they may be focusing on one aspect rather than integrating them all, day in and day out.

Mind – In this book, I refer to this skill as responding. This means that in moments of inner sensitivity, what's required is to renegotiate a new perception over the current situation through cognitive power words, questioning old perceptions, addressing our physiology, and even altering the way we listen to the thoughts in our head. Later on, in the responding chapter, I'll show you how this is done correctly and most effectively.

Body – Think about icky feelings in your body as stored memories that haven't been dealt with, like a folder on your desktop computer that pops open when you address one of those feelings. Through the power of reframing, we can locate the source of distress in the body, begin altering the perceptions over the events that have everything to do with the feeling, and change how the physical body feels as we discharge the stuck energy.

Spirit – Ask 100 people to give you an explanation about what spirit means, and you'll get 100 different answers. To me, spirit is the life force moving through us on the inside and communicating with everything on the outside.

We heal the spirit by making peace with peace

When the conscious and subconscious mind are working in positive harmony, the body reflects the positive result of that congruence. When all three are working in harmony, the spirit and life force within is healthy.

Since these core beliefs are the drivers to our emotional state and our identity, let's look into why you may find it so challenging to let go of some of them:

Certainty – You feel a sense of knowing what to expect in the future, even though you know these beliefs aren't healthy, nor do they help you to access your real capabilities.

147

Love & Connection – You may feel that if you let go of these core beliefs, you will create a deep disconnect between you and your parents, your siblings, your current family, friends, etc. This is unconscious, and rarely does a person come to this realization consciously.

Significance – It makes you feel like you're a somebody; you have a place in the world. Which actually goes against what you most likely felt for the majority of your childhood (many people feel insignificant). Again, this is at an unconscious level.

Contribution – You may feel like these beliefs help you to contribute toward others in some way. Maybe you've connected your stunning career to keeping these beliefs alive; maybe you feel that your spouse is with you due to the "brokenness" you share with them. If you feel you are contributing positively and that this contribution is connected to keeping your beliefs alive, you're setting yourself up for a steep uphill climb.

Uncertainty – The opposing beliefs come with too much uncertainty in terms of how you'll feel, how others will react to you, and so on.

Growth – You may feel like because you're growing in other aspects of your life, it has something to do with the beliefs you hold. Closely connected to contribution, this is again a delusional way of seeing the whole situation because your growth has nothing to do with your lack mindset, your fears, your unforgiveness, your anger, your guilt, or otherwise.

You are not your beliefs, but your beliefs have turned you into someone you believe you are. This is a turning point in your life as you move through the levels of beliefs and begin finding your true self once and for all.

Summary:

- You have two separate beliefs — your conscious beliefs and subconscious beliefs — and it's the subconscious beliefs that have manifested and grown through past and recent experiences that dictate your perceptions and how you feel.

- When changing core beliefs, we must respect that we will move through different forms/personalities, as well as respect the time it will take for healing.

- In change work, there must be an integration of the mind, body, and spirit for lasting change to take effect. These are all interconnected in terms of how one affects the other, but still must be practiced individually, if possible.

- Our core beliefs turn us into an artificial version of our true selves and keep us disconnected from our superconscious mind, which is responsible for the miracles we manifest in our lives.

- Almost every physical ailment has its roots in repressed emotions and core beliefs. When the emotional state of a person changes consistently, it brings with it the ability to physically heal from just about anything.

CHAPTER 12:

Health Anxiety Uncovered

"Beneath most symptoms of anxiety lies heartache."

This book wouldn't be complete without a chapter on health anxiety simply because I believe it's the fastest-growing "anxiety disorder" out there today. The longer we live, the more we will be bombarded by information that makes us feel that sickness is inevitable. You see it in posters, on TV, through the energy and words of others, in today's music, just about everywhere you look. If we don't become aware of this rising phenomenon, we may just be succumbing to the agendas of today's billion-dollar industries, which are more interested in us getting sick and keeping us sick.

Health anxiety is defined as a growing concern over having or developing a physical illness. It's a misrepresentation of feelings in and on the body (moles, scars, lines, bumps, etc.) that add to the sensitization that one feels daily. Health anxiety is a mental (thinking), emotional (feeling), and physical (being) issue that is formed by an unconscious imaginative process that is fed into through thought and action. The journey toward receiving the label of a health-anxiety sufferer could have come from anywhere. One traumatizing moment could have caused this deep sensitivity to your bodily sensations, or even consecutive experiences that constantly confirmed that a person must stay hyper-aroused just in case a physical illness was oncoming. This is what I call "standing guard." This habit presupposes that if the person stands guard at the doorway of their body through each and every moment of the day and reacts instinctively enough to anything that may feel "abnormal," they stay safe from potential danger. This is their safe zone, a mental jail cell with layer after layer of protective walls that keep away anything that seems unfamiliar and uncertain. This safe zone that health-anxiety sufferers cling to so tightly gives them the perception of protecting their survival. Soon enough, worry becomes a way of life, and the person's identity becomes deeply attached to fear.

Standing guard creates a constant constriction in the body that only strengthens bodily sensations. This connection goes unrecognized by the health-anxiety sufferer, though, since their only concern is to react impulsively to potential bodily danger. A consistently tense body is 100 times more stimulated by sound, smell, taste, sight, and physical touch (like bodily contact). This depth of sensitivity can also cause someone to interpret past events as worse than they actually were. With every similar reaction to a sensation or news from the outside, the stronger the health-anxiety identity becomes. Soon, this person will begin looking for opportunities to ask others whether a sensation in their body might be a serious physical ailment or not (reassurance seeking). Other people may brush it off quickly with words like "sounds normal to me, but just in case, you should get it checked out." The last part of that sentence sends the health-anxiety sufferer into a new level of frenzy, and then they are even less in tune with the outside and more internally tuned in to their bodily sensations.

It's tiring to be a health-anxiety sufferer. I should know, having spent 98% of 6 years having struggled with the cycle. The 2% when I didn't struggle was mostly due to alcohol, benzodiazepines, sex, or other distractions from being overly internal. There are four problems when it comes to health anxiety, and they are:

Judgments and opinions:

Take a look and see if you might be internalizing what someone else's view is about overall health. Have you accepted similar opinions and judgments as other authority figures or family members? It's best to ask yourself whether what you believe is causing you further health anxiety is your interpretation or from someone in your past or present.

Causal relationships:

This relates to predicting similar outcomes in the future to what took place in the past in such areas as panic, the flu, physical challenges, and other personal issues. Many health-anxiety sufferers believe that whatever happened will only happen again, and potentially much worse. So to stand guard would be a good option just in case something does go wrong, and they can catch it early enough to deal with it.

Identity misconception:

When we take on and accept the social labels that have been "assigned" to us, we eventually create a worried person within. This person, over time, begins to associate worry with protection from any further trouble that may show up. This level of identity misconception can be replaced with a new identity, as well as working toward defying one's irrational fears of ill-health daily.

Future pacing:

This is when a person has no particular focus on the present moment or what they're doing. They have an overly concerned mindset that rarely gives way to the conscious recognition of what their five senses are picking up in the moment. This can lead to a zombie-like existence for many. I used to label myself as a dead man walking, merely existing but not truly living.

Health-anxiety sufferers eventually feel their bodily sensations so deeply that they may wake up in the morning hoping the day flies by so that they can go back to sleep again. This is because sleep is the only time they aren't met with such deep sensitivity. They begin looking for ways to release themselves from feeling altogether. Since numbing the sensations will take away the emotional and physical pain, they begin abusing benzodiazepines, or even herbs in the hope of finding the off switch to their anxiety symptoms. (Herbs like ashwagandha, chamomile and valerian are great in moderation and as a sidekick to doing the inner work.) The harder they try, the more constricted their body becomes, the tighter their organs get, and the more shallow their breathing becomes, sending less oxygen to the brain. This is when you begin hearing about one of the most common reactions to health anxiety, dizziness.

Dizziness can produce more anxiety and more anxiety can produce more dizziness

Lightheadedness and dizzy spells can occur persistently or rarely. What's interesting about this symptom is that it can become much more noticeable when nothing is really going on. A person may be deeply engaged in a workout or a conversation with another person only to find themselves free from dizziness. While resting, for many health-anxiety sufferers, their systems may go into shock and bring them right back into hyper-arousal and full alertness in the hope of standing guard once again. Dizziness can lead to scattered thinking, which can cause tremendous difficulty when trying to concentrate on one thing (hence the challenges with meditation) as well as distort their long-term and short-term memory. The dizziness becomes a tool for the subconscious to keep the person fully engaged in fear, since fear was the earliest and most common message that was presented to their nervous system during childhood.

A lot of people are surprised to find that even when they are doing the deep inner work daily, there's still an unconscious attachment to dizziness. This is because the body is the last thing to recover. As previously mentioned, the biggest part of the subconscious mind is the body. The mind may reduce its attachment to catastrophic thinking and gravitate more toward pleasant future possibilities, the emotions may turn to neutral and even happy more often throughout the day, and a person's mental imagery may be much more pleasant, but the subconscious body hangs on for dear life as long as it can. This deters people from following through with the plan that's working for them. They believe they aren't making progress when, in fact, they're making tremendous progress, and it's just a matter of time before all these inner parts are back in harmony again.

It reminds me of a person deep within a mine digging for gold. They dig, and dig, and dig, as they get closer to the location of the gold on their map. And just before they're about to reach the reward they've been working so hard for, they quit and go back. Why go back? What do you have to lose by staying on the recovery path you're on? Nothing! But going back will lead you right back into the same health-anxiety cycle, and you'll only be labeling the recovery journey as "just not meant for you."

It's vital that we create a shift in consciousness if we are ever going to halt the rising number of health-anxiety sufferers around the world. A set mindset, which is closed off to new ideas and belief systems, won't get us there, but a growth mindset that's open to positive change will. The time has come to turn the victim mentality around and put health anxiety behind us once and for all. It's time to place more emphasis on trust and faith over survival since forceful action in the hope of longevity only lessens the quality of your life and potentially your lifespan as well. Health-anxiety sufferers must begin replacing the word "trigger" with "challenge." A trigger is seen as something to be avoided and keeps a person sensitized. A challenge, however, sees the stimuli as a log in a flowing river. This log can be moved through the RIC teachings so that the river can once again flow as it's meant to. No person goes through life without consistently having to remove logs from their own river. It's just how it is.

Here's the cycle that you normally see within a health-anxiety sufferer:

- Curiosity

Something in the outside world (a comment, image, etc.) or in the inside world (a feeling or sensation) creates curiosity within the person as to what it could mean. This doesn't naturally lead to the conscious mind looking for answers but the subconscious mind looking to replay what happened the last time the same situation occurred. The health-anxiety sufferer, at this moment, recognizes that his concerns are growing because of the unconscious attachment between concern and preventing the worst possible conclusion. The idea of letting it slide and not paying attention to it places too heavy a burden on the health-anxiety sufferer. Since the belief is that if a physical ailment does arise, they could have had a chance to prevent it from happening.

- NATS (negative automatic thoughts)

The thoughts begin coming in fast and relentlessly as one connects to the next (the spiderweb effect). The automatic imagination then kicks in, and the worst potential scenario comes to the forefront of the person's mind, thus strengthening the emotions in the body. The more emotions get involved, the more difficult it becomes to use rational thinking and logic to intercept the cycle and reverse it.

- Reassurance, avoidance, and fleeing

In this stage, the sufferer does whatever it takes to release themselves from what they're feeling. They ask their support person (usually the most-trusted member of their family or a friend) for reassurance over the idea that they aren't in imminent danger. They also look to avoid the immediate plans they've made or look for the exit door if they're already in a situation.

One of the keys to freedom from health anxiety (alongside reframing the experiences that are still being held onto by the subconscious) is to create awareness during the curiosity stage. Once this is done, the person can begin utilizing methods around responding to begin replacing and ridiculing their irrational thoughts, therefore placing a whole new meaning over what they're feeling.

If Generalized Anxiety is being highly focused on all the ways life could go wrong, Health Anxiety is being highly focused on all the ways the body could go wrong

"Why do you worry so much?" That was a question I got asked quite often throughout my life. At the time of my developmental years as a child, I would think to myself, "How do people live so freely?" It seemed like so many people had no concerns at all, flowing and gliding through life, paying no attention to potential bullying, detention, not getting homework done, making a fool out of yourself, being rejected by the cute girl you asked out, and more.

I eventually got really good at not showing my anxiety to others

Masking your anxiety doesn't mean it goes away, though, as you already know very well. It means that it just continues to grow deep down within you. Any past experiences that go unresolved will show up as bodily symptoms, reflexive thoughts, and mental images later in life. This is the way the subconscious mind tries to get the conscious mind's attention to see whether the time is right to place a new meaning over a past event. No conscious interaction and renegotiation over what took place means further repression of the emotions that go with that past experience.

Welcome to the hellish world of living with generalized anxiety followed by health anxiety

It doesn't end there, though. Since worrying is what highly sensitized people do, our brain's filter system does three very interesting things to make sure that the anxious meanings we've placed over ourselves and the world get fulfilled. Here's what the filter system of the brain does outside of our conscious awareness:

Deletions – The brain deletes information that isn't in line with the anxiety sufferer's core beliefs. So anytime "good" arises, the brain rejects the good and goes straight to the "bad."

Generalizations – The brain groups everything together into one huge anxious snowball. For example, you'll hear people say, "Nobody understands my anxiety," or "Life is a constant struggle." These generalizations fit nicely within the anxious template held in the subconscious of a sufferer. Putting this into health-anxiety terms, all bodily sensations (as well as illness-related information from the outside) must be taken as truth. This truth is a generalization that only gets strengthened the more anxious behaviors follow an anxious thought or feeling in the body.

Distortions – The brain alters information that's presented to you through your five senses so that it manipulates the safety within it, and emphasizes the dangers or threats. As an example, think about going to a grocery store. For an emotionally neutral person, this experience is a pleasant one full of goodies and healthy foods to pick up. But for an anxiety sufferer, that good information is bypassed, and the focus is turned solely onto all that could possibly go wrong between them and other people. For a health-anxiety sufferer, the symptoms could get too extreme during an experience like waiting in the checkout line. This has dire consequences to the sufferer in terms of their social life, and feelings of inner guilt, which lead to further self-punishment and future avoidance. Health-anxiety sufferers naturally distort information to fit with their health-anxiety identity and habitual viewpoints.

You can think of this system as a protection mechanism looking out for your own good. I always begged this system to look out for my own good less! But it didn't listen to my feedback much at the time. Let's dive in and look deeper into this very real and consistent transition from GAD to health anxiety that I've recognized in many people today.

Over-worrying will lead to a more sensitized physical body

Although the mind and body have different functions, they are one unit. They work together. This means that through the mental body, if a person has built up habits that pursue the catastrophic potentials in most of their day-to-day experiences, the body will begin responding as well. When the body starts responding through physical sensations, it can be easy for the mental body to misinterpret these bodily symptoms of anxiety and think that a physical illness is present; hence the result is health anxiety.

The transition from living, to feeling like the end is near

When a person begins forming associations between the physical sensations of anxiety and having or developing a physical illness, they may feel like their time on this planet is near the end. They may Google their symptoms of anxiety and convince themselves that the illness that they have is beyond them, and the feeling of hopelessness can arise. This is the day-to-day experiences of being in the mind, body, and spirit of someone whose generalized anxiety turns into health anxiety. The catastrophic scenarios in the external world, meet with the same possibilities in the internal world.

At this point in the transition from generalized anxiety to health anxiety, the fears aren't just related to people or situational challenges; there are bigger challenges going on within. The attention begins to get highly focused on the body, and the mind begins connecting one negative idea to the next. From here, a health-anxiety sufferer begins believing that their safety coping methods are the main strategy.

Health anxiety is a bundle of habits

If you think about it, you've always been a bit of a worrier. Worry has become the safety measure that keeps danger away from you (or so you think). It keeps life in the realm of certainty and keeps uncertainty at a distance. So, when generalized anxiety turns into health anxiety, it becomes obvious that it's a continuation of the anxious identity you believe you are.

I say this because many anxiety sufferers fear change; they fear inner peace and calmness as well because of how foreign it feels. People today feel like when they take time to relax that it's a waste of time and that they should be concerned over something or doing something. Welcome to the anxiety rat race!

It's best not to fall for this trap, and it's best not to place judgment on people who "do" less than you, and it's best not to value yourself based on how much you get done, what your occupation is, or how much worry you went through for the day. When generalized anxiety turns into health anxiety, it's vital that we see it as a growing sign of disconnect from inner peace.

To go against the anxious ideas that are playing out in the mind, and to act in accordance with the inner peaceful and balanced you is liberating!

In the end, you aren't your thoughts, you aren't your words, and you aren't your actions. Heck, you aren't even who you think you really are right now in your life! Who you are today is someone who has manifested a deep sense of sensitivity based on the desire to please others, expectations that weren't met, and experiences that caused overwhelm and helplessness within you. Remember that health anxiety is not a life sentence. The better your relationship gets with your physical sensations, the better it will get with your thinking, and vice versa. Since the fear of dying underlies health anxiety reactions, an acceptance over the cycle of life and death will lead to less mental and emotional engagement with bodily symptoms. When this happens, a person may find themselves in a gray area — a place where they fear dying less and begin pondering existential questions instead. This could cause a whole new batch of anxiety problems until complete faith in the unknown is restored. Because since it's the unknown that keeps a health-anxiety sufferer sensitized, it's also the change in heart toward the unknown that makes them desensitized.

Life and bodily sensations aren't supposed to be fought with; they are supposed to be worked with

The goal is to understand these sensations and the protective messages being sent out by the inner child. To achieve this goal, we must understand the cycle of life as we model our attitudes around the teachings of nature. The ocean doesn't fight with the rocks within it, the swaying branches on trees don't become frustrated by the wind that moves them, and the day does not fight with night for supremacy. It all flows with effortless synchronicity. It always has, and it always will. When we begin studying the ways nature works, we can begin to see how negatively distorted our core beliefs and behaviors have become.

How this all translates to health anxiety is by rejecting the fear that has been taught, and accepting the presence of good physical health, therefore positively affecting the mental, emotional, and spiritual bodies. Some people may feel that this is easier said than done, but these people are only held back by this belief, not by the process itself. The opposing idea that change can and has happened rapidly in the past fills them with a sense of discomfort since the subconscious programs around the need to self-punish to achieve are still very much alive. Nothing becomes a smooth ride; everything becomes more difficult due to how one views the challenges.

Self-hatred about health anxiety must be replaced with temporary acceptance of this mental and emotional state. This is where it all begins because further negative labels only fuel the fire of anxiety within. Having gentleness and compassion toward yourself while you temporarily go through health anxiety will bring up the answers needed for freedom, and they just might show up when they are least expected.

Summary:

- Health anxiety can manifest due to external worries and general anxiety; general anxiety can manifest due to internal worries and health anxiety. One can come before the other; many times, they go hand in hand throughout the day justifying their inner and outer fears.
- Health anxiety is a lack of accepting the flow of life provided by the teachings of nature. Instead, it's a fight to gain complete control and understanding over every bodily sensation and every catastrophic thought.

- There is no shame in health anxiety, and one big win emotionally throughout the day can shift the entire perceptions over a health-anxiety sufferer's inner fears.
- Reassurance seeking, Googling symptoms, leaning on other people consistently, and complete avoidance over outside environments that have the potential to cause further bodily reactions, must be stopped and reversed. Reassurance seeking must turn to communicating progress from the day, Googling symptoms replaced with studying your true purpose in life, leaning on others must be replaced with relying on your reframing and responding tools from this book, and avoidance behaviors must be progressively visited with the mindset that they are challenges, not potential triggers.

CHAPTER 13:

Emotional Abuse by Parents

*"You came to this world unique;
don't leave it as a copy."*

As we uncover the roots of your anxiety, you'll be met with voices from your parents and other authority figures; images from your past, and even physical pain related to past impacts. This should create further clarity within you so that you don't need to continue to force away what needs to be looked at directly. When I work with people through the reframing of memories, there are times when the subconscious prevents the information from showing up out of fear of expressing rather than further repression of the emotions. If this is the case, I go directly to the body and work there instead of with the memory. There is no part in the body that isn't capable of expressing the information connected to a person's past. We also used to believe that all memories were only stored in the brain until we realized that the heart and the gut are also processors. Many times, the gut is referred to as the second brain.

Childhood emotional abuse by a parent or other figure is devastating for a child. The parent doesn't see the situation from the mind and body of the child, and the effects of this emotional abuse can show up many years down the road. The child, when presented with art therapy, regularly turns to the colors red (pain and violence) and black (no safety) to begin painting a picture of what their emotional or physical abuse looks like to them. When a child is asked to color a picture of something pleasant in their lives, they regularly turn to the colors white and blue. These colors are attached to the child's perceptions. Having worked with many adults and children over the years, I've recognized the power of color in shifting perceptions. Try this right now:

- Get comfortable where you are and take a deep breath
- Locate a part of your body where you're holding fear and give it a color
- Now think about what your safety color would be — the color that makes every situation better
- Start with an exhale, breathing out the color of fear, and for five repetitions breathe in the color of safety to that area of your body, followed by breathing out more of your fear color

Notice how you feel after only five repetitions. Most people say they experience a slight or dramatic shift in their emotional state, and as their day goes on, a shift in the way they perceive what they fear. These are the types of languages that I'll discuss from time to time to give you an idea of how we communicate with ourselves at the deepest levels of our being. I bet you only thought it was thoughts; little did you realize it's colors, sounds, vibrations, and more.

Childhood emotional abuse can feel like physical abuse even though no hand was ever laid on a child

Also, sometimes, when the adult recalls the emotionally abusive memory, he or she believes they were physically abused even though they weren't. That's how bad it was for them. A major problem here is that most children blame themselves for the way their parents treated them. They feel like somehow they deserved to be treated in such a way. This is an attempt to regain some sense of control and power.

Emotionally and physically abused children not only feel that their behaviors were wrong, but their very existence in this world is wrong. Think about that for a second. The child's sense of self is lost; they're completely in the dark throughout the day and attracting more chaos into their systems at every turn. To understand this better, we must realize that children are egocentric, meaning they believe that everything revolves around them. So most of the good that happens is because of them, and also the bad, in their minds.

See where your childhood may have fit in with these five behavioral forms of emotional abuse.

Isolating

This is when the parent prevents the child from participating in normal childhood activities. This could be sporting events, playground activities, or even keeping the child from interacting with other children of certain ethnicities. Within the parent, there's an obvious sense of losing something if the child is left to interact as they please. Many isolating parents have experienced great loss in their lives in terms of other people they cared for, and they want to make sure they keep the child all to themselves, just in case the child makes them #2 instead of #1.

Words hold tremendous power behind them and anyone on this journey toward healing must realize the importance of changing the vocabulary within their inner dialogue, and with others. Parents who isolate their children frequently use the words "be careful" with their kids. Even when the child gets to do something he or she would like to do, a sense of danger gets inserted into their mind and body. "Be careful," means "be afraid," and it's an unconscious way of pulling the child back into the comfort zone of the parent.

If the child finds that they are afraid during an experience, and feels overwhelmed or uncomfortable, they will likely begin adopting the view that the parent has over them and the world. As the child continues absorbing the message to be careful, their survival brain, which takes in the five senses, relays more and more threatening information back to the emotional brain, which then signals to the body to get revved up by secreting adrenaline throughout the system. Then, a harmless event turns into a life-threatening scenario all because of the words "be careful."

The reverse of this, should the isolating parent recognize how limiting an existence the child is really going through and the fact that the parent must resolve their subconscious fears, are the words "be aware." When "be aware" gets uttered, the child is in more of a neutral emotional place, interpreting the world as it is and not worse than it is. As the words "be aware" enter into the mind of the child, the child begins strengthening his or her conscious resources, therefore analyzing rather than reacting frantically, and using logic rather than succumbing to catastrophic future ideas.

Isolating parents will fight to the death to justify why they do what they do with their child. They believe so firmly that isolation is vital because the world can't be trusted. If you're currently on this boat as a parent, when did you lose that trust? It never matters what happened to you as a child, only what you decide to do about it now. Isolation may provide a sense of doing the right thing as a parent for the child, but in the end, the child will grow up with a tremendous lack of social skills and a lowered self-image, simply because he or she never had the opportunities to live and learn.

Ignoring

This is when the parent (or another caregiver) is psychologically unavailable to the child and fails to respond to the child's behavior. In many cases, the parent just can't seem to break out of the mental fog that they are in due to a deep sense of overwhelm and total depletion. Learned helplessness is ever-present. Kids who excessively use mobile phones and iPads for games could very well have an ignoring parent since the device is the babysitter, and the parent can be left alone. I'm thankful that I never had ignoring parents, but I can attest to going through some of the other emotional abuses laid out here.

What's important with ignoring, and these other aspects of parenting, isn't so much to place blame on the parents and caregivers as it is to come from a more compassionate and understanding place. The question we always want to ask is, "why does a person do what they do?" Also, the person must feel like it's a problem before they'll do anything about it. If little Johnny is constantly fighting for mom's attention, and mom's on Facebook scrolling through her newsfeed trying to catch up with everyone else's lives, it's a problem to onlookers. But to mom, the need for this type of connection outweighs the connection she feels she can always have with the child the moment she asks for it. The authority figure must be long-term focused rather than short-term focused.

Often, we don't recognize the consequences of our actions until we spend more time on how we can improve the mental environment in the home. Once a parent recognizes what path the child may be on through consistent ignoring, they may begin attaching more pain to their behaviors. Human beings do what they do to avoid pain and gain pleasure. So, if there's something not happening at the moment that needs to happen, the pain of doing it could be very real and ever-present, which outweighs the pleasure. I know what you're thinking, "how could there possibly be pain attached to the parent fulfilling a child's needs?" Here are a few core beliefs that might be present within the parent:

- By not responding, I bypass more responsibility, and since I'm overwhelmed, this is the way I can deal with this right now.
- The less I respond, the better chance that the child will leave me alone in the future, and I'll gain my sense of self again.
- Through ignoring, I feel a sense of significance and power over my child. I get to choose when my attention is given and when it's not. I'm the one in charge, and my attention isn't given as easily as the child wants.

We begin to see what's really taking place at the core of the authority figure because the truth is that there's no such thing as a bad behavior. The behavior might not be acceptable to others, but it sure does a good job of protecting the subconscious programs that are running in the person's head. The only person it has to make sense to is the parent, that's all. The calling to fulfill the core beliefs of the parent overtakes the need from the child and becomes justified in their conscious minds. The parent may say, "can't you see I'm busy!" or "tell me about it later." Of course, the reaction could have been completely different, and a deeper bond could have taken place, but even that may bring up some fear within. Many ignoring parents have also grown up being ignored themselves. Since children mirror their parents' behaviors, it very well could be a generational pattern that goes on and on. That is until someone does something about it, and consistently.

Corrupting

This is when the caregiver urges the child to learn false values that reinforce antisocial or deviant behavioral patterns such as aggression, substance abuse, or criminal acts. Remember that the outcome of who the child will become as an adult and what they will believe depends heavily on what takes place between the age of 0-5 years. Take a sponge, for example. When does the sponge absorb the most water? When it's new and dry, of course. The same goes for the mind, body, and spirit of a human being. The messages around corrupting could come in many different ways, such as "fight authority," "people can't be trusted," or "you must take what you want because the world's not going to give it to you."

As the child begins mirroring the behavior of the most important developmental figures in their lives, they begin becoming them; they are a carbon copy in pretty much every way. There's also a big discussion going around today whether video games are corrupting children. To that, I would have to ask, "who took the time and spent the money to buy these video games for the child in the first place?" Video games today are subliminally programming kids in ways that create extraordinary fear and rage within. Parents must understand this and gradually begin cutting down video game time and replacing it with new habits. The problem is that the video game creates such a surge of dopamine that once the child is off the screen, everything else feels like the volume's been turned down, it's all lame. The more they play, the more levels they pass, and the more the need for the same level of excitement arises. And so when you put a book in the child's hands, it doesn't come with as much reward as the video game does, not even close.

Corrupting parents fail to teach their children right from wrong. Many caregivers also reward the child for harassing behavior or even bullying in some way, seeing it as a way of proving power and strength over others. Racism and ethnic biases are also prevalent in today's world. The less reward a child sees emotionally, verbally, and materialistically, the less they'll want to engage in this kind of behavior. But at this level of conditioning, if the caregiver doesn't see it as a problem, neither will the child, so it must start with the parent or caregiver.

Terrorizing

Terrorizing means to inflict severe punishment or deliberately create an environment of fear. I'll give you a good example of this:

A child is about to play in a tennis tournament (who could this be?). The warming up for the match begins 3 hours earlier as the child gets the message that if a loss happens, it will be devastating for the parents and the child's future. The child hits 4,000 tennis balls in the hope of being mentally, emotionally, and physically ready for the match. The parent reminds the child that they must win by any means possible, which creates a conflict of interest in the child's mind briefly. The child goes into the match as the caregiver paces frantically in the background. The pressure mounts within and all the child's abilities disappear due to an imbalance going on with the emotions. Mentally, the child stops thinking and begins reacting as the screams get louder from the parent, and now the personal coach arrives as well. The match ends with a loss. The parent and coach are nowhere to be found. The child spends the next 20 minutes waiting in great distress as to if or when the parent will show up to take him home. The parent doesn't show up, so the child gets a ride from a family friend instead. As the car drops the child off in front of his apartment, the shaking begins, and the child asks the family friend to come up with him, but the family friend is too busy. Anything is possible from here.

It's no accident, in this case, that the child grew up with a sense of dread everywhere he looked. It was also very much of a pleasing game, so this person would do all they can to avoid any conflict since that's all they experienced as a child. Personally, it was very challenging for me to completely put my terrorized past behind me just by consciously going about it. Responding and altering my thinking patterns brought me some relief and helped me see a new point of view behind who was terrorizing me at the time. Although, for a long time, I never fully felt I could move past it. It was like a black cloud that followed me everywhere, not allowing me to experience a sense of calm and inner peace for long. I realized that the responding part in moments of thinking and feeling "badly" had to be connected with reframing. Because what reframing did for me is it helped me to say and do what I couldn't say or do at the time. I expressed myself loudly, I punched pillows, I cried, and I felt a sense of stepping out of the boundaries others had set for me, which was the real key to my freedom.

This is why CBT (cognitive behavioral therapy) practices alone may not be able to get to the root of the problem and solve it. Simply because this inner wounded child that we go about our day getting information from needs to be provided with an outlet over the reasons they repressed their emotions. The fear needs to be destroyed, the caregiver needs to be told how wrong their attitudes and teachings were, and many times the person reframing might even need to knock the caregiver out in their imagination, not in real life. Whatever it takes. Because terrorizing has no place in a child's life; it's wrong, plain, and simply wrong. No child should ever feel like their presence in this world was a mistake, and that's just what terrorizing does.

Rejecting

Rejecting is a refusal to show affection as well as behaviors that communicate abandonment to the child. We briefly touched on this in the chapter, but it's vital to see if your current distress could be connected to this in your upbringing. This is an important connection to make so that you can have an explanation as to why you feel what you feel and why you do what you do. The understanding itself may not be enough to reorganize your identity and place a new meaning over life, but it can lead to the answers you seek.

Many adults reject positive feedback, bodily contact, and even self-loving thoughts due to an underlying belief around rejecting, and that it's the right way of doing things. The child who feels this level of rejection may find it very difficult to share what's going on with others, due to not wanting to be an even bigger burden on other people. Their self-confidence shrinks as they just can't seem to piece together what they did wrong to initiate the lack of love from their caregivers.

A deep sense of loss follows this person daily as they go through their life. The more distracted they become in their adult lives, through work and other things, the farther away they get from being able to access the root cause for their sense of loss and shift its meaning. You can see how this inner need looks to get fulfilled by present relationships. I've consistently asked people, "Why are you in a relationship?" Their answer is usually, "Because I feel loved and can give love." The need gets met as the adult through the relationship; it's not so much that the other person is their soul mate or anything like that, but the inner wounded child gets what was needed.

Many times we do things in the present to fill the void left over from our past, without realizing it

People today want to get rich not because of financial freedom, but to feel more worthy. Others want to move to a new location on an island somewhere away from all the chaos not because they want a new experience, but to see if they can run away from themselves. They think that if they can change their environment, everything else on the inside will change. I'm sorry to burst that bubble though because this isn't an environmental issue; it's at the level of a core belief and identity issue. At an unconscious and conscious level, you have painted a vivid picture of yourself, and you're just fulfilling the traits that go along with the identity you were conditioned to be.

Summary:

- What happened to you isn't important; what's important is what you do about it and how you perceive it now.
- Forgiveness must take center stage here. It wasn't your parents' or other authority figures' fault since they were doing the best they could with the information they had.
- The best thing about the past is that it's over.
- Recognize how you may be meeting the needs leftover from childhood today but in a negative way.
- Make sure you take note of whether you're continuing with your own children the same patterns you experienced as a child from your parents. This realization alone comes with a level of deep insight that can turn your behaviors around.

CHAPTER 14:

Trauma-Based Anxiety

"Trauma occurs, your perceptions freeze, the entire experience gets stored in a part of your body, and the oatmeal in your stomach in that moment becomes an unknown trigger for the future."

Trauma is defined as a deeply distressing or disturbing experience. In my experience working with many anxiety sufferers, the current conscious or unconscious sensitivity that they have in any potential situation is due to one of two possibilities:

> A single event that was highly distressing that caused the person to unconsciously initiate the freeze/helpless response, and one where the conscious mind was too overwhelmed to intervene.

> Or multiple events that caused a similar physiological freeze response.

Whether a person's current sensitivity and anxiety are due to a single event or multiple events doesn't matter. The energetic blockages within the body today are based on the inability to fight back, say your peace, release the anger, or run from or escape the situation during those moments in the past. Instead, what happened was there was hyperarousal, a freezing sensation, constriction in the body, and dissociation (a feeling of not being present, slow motion, or other uncommon experiences).

Many people today are misinformed about the fight or flight response, the mechanism within us that responds quickly to an external threat (or an imagined one). The fight or flight response, as seen in all animals, is a very valuable inner mechanism. Within the animal kingdom, when the response is activated, it can mean the difference between escape or being eaten alive. If a human goes through an experience, has a fight or flight activation, and follows through with either verbally or behaviorally fighting or escaping the situation, the emotions either don't get locked in the body at all or very little. It is not labeled a full emotional trauma. If, however, the person helplessly freezes, feels overwhelmed, experiences an inability to respond, feels a deep level of constriction in the body and experiences an uncommon phenomenon such as an out-of-body experience, the experience is labeled a full trauma within the RIC teachings. The process looks like this:

- Hyperarousal – A physiological response to an overwhelming event
- An unsuccessful escape, and or an inability to physically or verbally fight back
- The experience of total helplessness and overwhelming fear
- Complete immobility (freezing) and a deep sense of shock

Whenever a threatening situation occurs, we regularly turn for help and social support at that moment to help with the distress. During this initial reaction, while hyperaroused, we seek the support of others to help. If no one is present to support us, our limbic system (emotional brain) turns on, and the sympathetic nervous system takes over. This response decreases the amount of responsiveness we have toward the voice of another person as we've automatically turned off the ability to engage socially with others and our sensitivity to the external sounds other than voice increases. The organism shuts down to use up as little internal resources and energy as possible, and we move into a state of inner collapse. Our gut seizes up, our breathing becomes shallow, and our metabolism drastically reduces. At this point, the person begins temporarily (and many times much longer) moving into a state of depersonalization, which is feeling as if you're living inside a bubble, disengaged from the outside world and your sensory systems.

One of the most challenging things for trauma victims is to confront their shame over the way they reacted during the traumatic experience

This is natural and can be put behind for good. In my personal experiences with trauma, the after-effects hit me hard and instantly. I was emotionally numb for many years; it altered my perceptions and my imagination to the point of such distress that each day I thought I was going crazier and crazier. I had lost total control of my body, my thinking, and even my behaviors. People around me kept downplaying the severity of what I was going through, and I had come to a very interesting conclusion about my post-trauma experiences that had led to my anxiety disorder — my body didn't know I was out of the past trauma. This was a revelation to me at the time and in how I approach my clients going through present anxiety. It made complete sense. Since my system had grouped everything together in the environment and took a picture of the experience just prior to the peak intensity of the moment, everything around me was labeled a threat and dangerous to my survival. Therefore, as I went about my days, I unconsciously scanned the environment, picking up threat after threat. Heck, even getting out of bed was a threat since a few of my traumatic experiences were around the stairs at my home, and my system desperately wanted me to stay in bed and not go down those stairs.

Everything in the external — everything — has some effect on a person's internal environment. Good or bad. Because most of our traumas took place so early on in our lives, though, it hides outside of our conscious awareness. That's where your symptoms come into play. Every mental, emotional, or physical symptom is a question and a statement. The question is:

"Are you sure you want to do that?"

And the statement is:

"Stay out of what you are about to do. You might make the same mistake you did last time, and feel the same overwhelming distress again."

My life began changing once I began responding to, rather than reacting to, these questions and statements. My normal reaction was to get frustrated by the intrusive thought, place guilt on myself for the emotional response that many times came out of nowhere (let alone repress even more rage in my body), and fear the physical symptom thinking death was right around each corner. I began understanding the power of opposites. I just started doing the opposite of what I had normally done within the initial stages of my distress and found myself engaged more in the outer world than my inner world. This was a key piece in my healing.

It's vitally important that we understand our symptoms, and don't place such harsh critical judgments on them when they arise. It's also important to ask the right questions to yourself in your inner dialogue as you go through your day. The right questions will expose what is being held within the subconscious mind-body. Questions like, "Why does this always happen to me?" will leave you in a state of further learned helplessness. Questions like, "What is this symptom trying to tell me?" or, "Why does my inner wounded child still feel wounded at this moment?" will open the floodgates to deep clarity and self-love. In the end, you really have to choose between the two main emotions, fear or love. Choose fear, and you live a delusional life thinking you need to tiptoe through life "just in case;" choose love, and you become aligned with nature's laws and a flow state within is reached.

With reframing, we're not looking to change your history, rather show the nervous system that the experience is over and provide safety over what took place. For us to effectively do this, we must go back to the times in your life when you learned the quickest and most effectively, your childhood. When you were a child, two things led to storing an experience into your long-term memory: One was your imagination, and the other was your emotions.

Remember when you were a child, and you put on your Spiderman costume and walked down the street looking for ways to help the community? You pretended you could fling spiderwebs through your wrists and swing from building to building. You were emotionally engaged, and there was no difference between the real Spiderman and you! Do this for a moment for me. Hold your arms up in victory for a 2-minute period, and recall a time in your life when you were extremely proud of something you did. Take your time; don't read on until the 2 minutes are up.

Now ask yourself, how absorbed was I during this short and powerful 2-minute exercise? Was I engaged in what I was doing, or did I allow my mind to wander into expectations of it not working? The level of absorption you have will dictate how much you get out of your reframing process. Second, ask yourself, how playful was I during this 2-minute exercise? Did I allow myself to play, or did I find it silly because of a core belief that showed up saying, "I'm too old for this stuff?" Jesus reminded us to "be as little children," and we should take that advice to heart. Because without your ability to be childlike again, you'll never overcome anxiety. This is because becoming childlike is to embrace uncertainty, to welcome it in and imagine positive outcomes, to be more carefree and less strict, and to see the world openly rather than just through the mind of your parents and past authority figures.

Reframing not only emphasizes the imaginative aspect but the somatic one as well. During a reframing experience, I'll ask my client to locate where in their body they're holding their fear, guilt, blame, or other emotion. I will also ask them to tell me the color of it (our first language out of the womb, which differentiated what was good from bad in the outside world, is color), the sound of it, if it has a sound, the shape of it ... even the direction it's spinning. These are all languages that the nervous system uses to encode the emotion. If we alter the languages, such as the color, the sound, the direction it's spinning, and the shape of it, we are literally speaking in metaphors, which is the language of the subconscious mind. So here's what we know so far about reframing:

- It emphasizes the use of the imagination, along with addressing the location of the distress that is being held within the body.
- It uses the infinite languages that the nervous system uses to keep an experience and emotion locked in the mind and body. Languages we use to alter the encoded information are the color, sound, and size of that particular stuck energy.
- It takes a high level of absorption, and childlike playfulness for the emotions to arise during the experience. These emotions are the very things that alter the perceptions over the memory and release the "negative" unconscious associations that cause a person to experience anxiety in the present.
- The power behind reframing is in its consistent use. Sometimes one reframing process might not be enough to discharge the emotions locked in the body and the perceptions locked in the mind, so relentless practice is essential until the person feels a natural emotional shift throughout the day.

In the next chapter, we'll be diving deep into this skillset, which is the reason for so many people's freedom from anxiety today. But in terms of the reason for reframing, which now we know comes down to traumatic memories, we must also understand the impact of generational trauma. The study in epigenetics research (studying the changes that happen in the expression of genes without modifying the actual sequences within the gene) provides us real evidence that intergenerational trauma is a very real phenomenon. We now know that children of PTSD-stricken mothers are three times more likely to struggle with anxiety and depression or engage in substance abuse when either parent had PTSD. It's not only what we inherit from our parents but also how they were parented that influences how we relate to a partner, ourselves, and how we nurture our children. Family members unconsciously repeat the sufferings of their past family members; this is commonly known as entanglement.

What does this mean in terms of our complete healing from anxiety using reframing and responding? According to Dr. Bruce Lipton, it means that when we can reframe our early traumatic experiences, we're ending the generational trauma cycle up to seven generations back, and seven generations forward. Ending your anxiety doesn't just bring you freedom; it provides an increased opportunity for your future family line to build on your inner progress over anxiety as well.

Summary

- Early childhood trauma can affect our current perceptions, personality, emotional states, and actions.
- Many people aren't aware that generational or personal past trauma has led to their anxiety cycle

in the present time. This is until someone brings it to their attention, works with them to relax the mind and body prior to re-experiencing and reframing their traumatic memories in a safe and effective manner.

- The way we view our memories can change depending on many factors in the present moment, such as how we feel, how exhausted we are, how much we take on daily, etc. This leads us to the understanding that our memories can certainly be perceptually altered, leaving us thinking that it was worse than what it really was.

- Trauma symptoms can show up through fear-based thinking patterns, repressed emotions that move into physical symptoms, and in other ways. These are always questions and statements presented to you by your inner wounded child, still looking to see whether the same meaning over the situation should stay, or if a new meaning is possible.

- Metaphors, emotion, and imagination are the languages of your subconscious mind. Utilizing these three during a reframing practice will give us a big advantage in reframing our memories and moving forward with our lives.

CHAPTER 15:

Reframing: The Secret Weapon To Healing Anxiety

"Unhealthy fear doesn't go away until you prove to your body that the event that triggered the fear is over."

I have to be honest with you, the first few weeks of guided reframing (prior to non-guided reframing) that I did with my mentor was hell. Hell, because I was facing what I had stuffed deep down within me — the experiences I wanted to put behind me, but that were instead showing up daily as bodily symptoms and other emotional problems. I just knew at the time that something was missing in my healing toolbox. I was working on changing my thinking, altering my perceptions, and exposing myself to what I feared, but I wasn't getting to where I wanted to go, which was inner freedom. That is until I was introduced to reframing and did it ever alter the path I was on. That's because, for a long time, I thought that whatever took place in the past was set in stone, the meaning and the emotions toward those events were locked in forever. Little did I realize at the time that how we perceive our past can change, forgiveness can be cemented, and our emotions toward those past events can be altered.

This concept both excited me and scared me at the same time. It excited me because I could once and for all release myself from the labels I had placed on myself, and the blame I had placed on others. It scared me because I didn't know how my mind and body would react to these changes in the moment, and later on after the process. The inner battle didn't last long; however, as I quickly let myself know that without discomfort, there would be no lasting change. Everything I had ever achieved in my life, from my career, to my relationships, to adopting new spiritual beliefs all had varying degrees of discomfort that came with them at the beginning. I was determined that I wasn't going to lie in my deathbed many years from now, uttering the words, "I wish I would have just taken that leap of faith and embraced the discomfort." Heck no! I had a life to live here, and anxiety wasn't going to suck it out of me anymore. I was determined to not only be as free on the inside as I used to be, but even freer! I wanted consistent inner peace and a pleasant life, and I knew I was on the right track with reframing and responding.

Reframing is an acronym for:

> R – **Renegotiate** the past experience (recent or earlier childhood memories)
> E – **Exit** the old perceptions
> F – Gain **forgiveness** for yourself and others
> R – **Release** repressed energy
> A – **Accept** the changes at a heart level
> M – **Mentally** refresh (start anew)
> E – **Emotionally** renew

During my anxiety disorder, I was highly depersonalized, dizzy, my memory and concentration were failing me, and I had a "tired but wired" feeling every day. I now realize that responding alone may not be enough to put anxiety behind for good. This is due to the person needing to fully be able to look back on their childhood and experience it in an emotionally neutral manner, and take the lessons needed for the present. I thought that because I had consciously forgotten about those past traumatic events that I was free from them. Little did I realize at the time that the subconscious mind and body never forget, although they do have the ability to reshape the meaning placed over any event.

We must get back in touch with the main ingredient that unlocks the path toward your healing, and that is depth. We must go deep into a world of uncertainty within the process of reframing so that responding in the moments of mental, emotional, physical, or imaginative distress becomes more effortless and comes with more reward. I began getting addicted to the process, I did it relentlessly, and the stored energy within my body started discharging little by little.

These are the three ways you store trauma in your mind and body:

- You remember the event and the feeling, you had no idea what to do with it, so you added more and more items to your to-do lists each day to push it aside. You thought you dealt with it, but those past experiences stay unresolved, and the pressure mounts over time.

- You store the photo of the event and lose your ability to feel. You become chemically protected as your body went into and stayed in a state of shock, and repressed all the feelings.
- The event, along with the feelings, moves straight to the subconscious mind and body within seconds of the event, and you have absolutely no memory of it happening. The body remembers, but the mind doesn't (as Dr. Bessel Van der Kolk puts it so beautifully in the title of his book "The Body Keeps the Score."

The longer a subconscious thought has been accepted, the more difficult it becomes to overcome through conscious intervention

To understand your present anxiety better, it's important to note that the same brainwave patterns show up when the memory of the event shows up. For example, holding a glass of water and feeling anxious makes no sense to the conscious mind, but to the subconscious mind, water might equal a threat if it's tied to a past traumatic experience. This is also why so many anxiety sufferers have trouble meditating. This is due to the subconscious literally saying, "if you relax too much, you might die," which leads us to always feeling like we must be on high alert, and inner peace is rarely ever experienced.

Most anxiety sufferers admit that they had a chaotic childhood, but implement responding skills in the present without reframing. This is why they find themselves never fully being able to accept a new, more neutral-to-pleasant meaning over a situation. Remember that healing anxiety is a convincing game. You must, on a daily basis, understand how to communicate with the deeper side of yourself and promote safety over experiences that have occurred in your past if you want to heal fully.

In reframing, five key components must be met during each practice. They are:

- **Basic regression** – Safely bringing a person back to a time in their lives when they believe they first experienced the freeze response and tremendous fear. Don't get caught up in whether it's the initial sensitizing event or not; just trust your first impression, go with it, and over time more missing pieces of information related to your current anxiety will show up.
- **Vent the emotional charge related to the event** – A complete discharge of the emotion/energy that has been lying stagnant over the years in the body. Our goal is to experience lightness after the process. Expressing verbally and behaviorally what you believe you should have done is a crucial step in no longer repressing the emotions.
- **Desensitize the event** – This is where a person no longer feels fearful toward the past situation. Instead, they feel a sense of emotional neutralness, and increased empowerment; they also begin questioning the freezing that took place before. When you desensitize from the event, as mentioned earlier, missing pieces of information start showing up throughout the day (in RIC teachings we call these "moments of clarity"), and we begin to open ourselves up to seeing the experience from different angles.

- **Receive forgiveness from yourself or others** – Getting forgiveness for what you or others did, or didn't do, is essential because so much anxiety in the present is due to tremendous guilt, shame, and repressed rage.
- **Reprocess the experience** – Completely altering how you perceive the event so that you feel the change, and not only think it has changed.

I hope that you can start seeing how all of this adds up. We are what we are today due to what we've kept locked in for too long. I'm completely convinced now, at this stage of my life, that the body is 100% memory.

Physical disease is almost 100% related to the volcano within that implodes over time, rather than being discharged in a safe and effective manner

Reframing is not denial. It doesn't deny the experiences of your past. It is re-evaluating those experiences to bring about a different outlook, therefore a different emotional response to it. We must begin learning how to use our imagination positively, and when we can engage in the somatic component — locating the parts in the body where the memories and feelings are stuck — we have a great opportunity for lasting change.

Anxiety makes you feel like you have to settle for less than what you truly want in life. You start making excuses about why it's not the right time to commit to change and tell yourself that you've suffered too long already to reverse anxiety for good. Here's the truth: The length of time you've suffered has nothing to do with how long recovery might take. I know that for a fact because I see it on a daily basis in my world.

There's no better time than now to start living the life you deserve to live. So decide, day one, or one day? I know you chose day one, so let's get into the script for reframing daily, which you can also download and begin using at http://www.theanxietyguy.com/reframing.

It's always recommended that you work with either an RIC coach, Hypnotherapist, Neuro-Linguistic Programming (NLP) practitioner, or Holographic Memory Resolution (HMR) coach who specializes in regression work, at least at the beginning of your journey. These are my best recommendations for this type of work, and reframing through RIC is a representation of all of them along with a few small alterations.

Below is a simple script for a gentle approach to healing and emphasizes a mild trance state, since you'll be highly conscious and using your body in some parts as well. Remember, again, to download the entire reframing experience as part of your anxiety-healing journey at http://www.theanxietyguy.com/reframing, and use it daily.

Relaxation induction - Take three deep breaths, focus on relaxing your eyelids, and let that relaxation flow from the top of your head down to the tips of your toes.

Physically point to the area in your body where you think you're storing the emotional distress (always go with your first impression).

As the adult-you looking in at the younger-you, how old might you have been when you first felt this level of fear, freezing sensations, and overwhelm?

Is the younger-you inside or outside?

Is it light or dark?

Who's around the younger-you?

What's happening as you analyze the experience from your current, adult perspective (detailed explanation)?

As the present-you, walk directly toward the younger-you and give that younger-you the biggest hug he/she has ever received. Take all the time you need to allow the emotions to come up and out in this moment as you rub the back of the younger-you.

Look into his/her eyes and tell them the truth about who they are, what they deserve, and what they have to look forward to. Let them know that this experience wasn't their fault, as well as anything else you believe that younger-you needed to hear at the time, but didn't.

Now have the younger-you express what he/she needs to express verbally and do what he/she wishes they would have done in that moment. If they could release what they suppressed, what would they do? Go ahead and give the younger-you permission to do that now and take as much time as you need to discharge what needs to be discharged.

What else does the child need to do to feel even safer in that experience?

Anything else?

Now ask the younger-you to communicate forgiveness either toward themselves or anyone else, for the child's sake and no one else's.

Now take a picture in your mind's eye of that moment of complete safety and empowerment that the child is experiencing right now so that anytime you look back and remember this experience, you remember it in a way that makes you feel safe.

Now think about the safest color that comes to mind, and spread that safety color around the frame of that picture now.

Take 10 deep breaths in and out slowly as you breathe in that safety color to the part of your body where you used to hold the fear and breathe out the old color of distress on every exhale now.

At this point, you will begin hearing a certain sound slowly showing up inside. This sound acknowledges your healing and provides lightness and inner peace to you now. Take your time, listen to this sound, and lose yourself in it now.

When I count to 5, your eyes will open, lightness will come over you, and any emotions that need purging and releasing will be let out. Old programming will be replaced with new, updated programming; don't question it, just fully accept the transition now as you allow your body to do whatever it wants to do to discharge what's left of the old fearful energy now.

1, 2, 3, 4, 5 open your eyes.

On a piece of paper, write down all the lessons you learned and want to keep from this experience. Write as much as you can so you can keep the lessons and let everything else go.

Think of reframing as going back into the time machine of your mind and moving through those past experiences where you froze in a different way. If you could have another chance to make that experience the way you wanted it to go, say and do what you wish you would have, and leave the experience feeling safe, how would it go?

As you can see in the script, you're the adult looking in on the younger version of yourself going through the discharging and forgiveness process. I believe this avoids retraumatizing the person should they live the experience out again in the first person. Instead, looking at the experience as the adult-you places the inner child in a very confident place to be able to say and do what they need to do. Sometimes I'll have my clients place a pillow on their laps during the process in case they want to punch the pillow as they're verbalizing and discharging. There's no Mr. Nice Guy during the process of reframing memories; it all comes out naturally. Taking the picture at the end replaces the old trauma-based picture, shifting all the other fear-based associations of that past experience (sometimes instantly; sometimes over time and with more practice).

What you should expect after a reframing experience is clarity. Throughout the following weeks (after daily practice), more and more epiphanies start showing up. Permission to alter a person's core beliefs and identity get recognized, confidence in new and more empowering ideas gets strengthened, and life begins feeling different. As long as the person doesn't sabotage this progress by falling victim to the ideas of "it won't last," or "these feelings are too unfamiliar," the new personality gets strengthened and cemented.

In reframing, if we project safety over the memory and talk to the memory, we can shift the physiological patterns connected with it. In my trauma work, I've also found that massage, meditation, and bodywork can help to consciously remember memories in order to reframe them. As a side note, benzodiazepines will mess with memory access and reframing; antidepressants, on the other hand, generally don't interfere with emotional reframing work (always work with your doctor on any changes you want to implement regarding medication).

Summary:

- Reframing is a tool to be used alongside responding for daily progress over anxiety.
- Reframing is used for past traumatic memories. The script above is an introduction to what I actually use with my clients in many of my 1-on-1 sessions.
- When we can communicate with the subconscious mind in a language it understands (emotion and imagination), we can begin to alter the meaning over past traumas directly. This creates a physiological shift in the present day.
- To put anxiety behind you once and for all, you must deal with it at the root, not through the symptoms. If we deal with anxiety at the symptom level, new symptoms will inevitably

reappear. This is what I like to refer to as the water-balloon effect, wherein an effort to release the water from the balloon (the symptoms), you squeeze it only to see them reappear in a different location. If we handle our anxiety at the root, meaning the initial and subsequent events that strengthened our fear-based perceptions, we regain our lost source of power.

- Change may be challenging to accept at the beginning fully. Over a short period of time, with continued relentless practice in reframing and responding, you will become much more comfortable in your new skin.

CHAPTER 16:

Anxiety & Panic Attacks

"People don't HAVE panic attacks; they unintentionally make themselves panic."

The experience of an anxiety or panic attack is something so terrifying that it can literally bring you to your knees. As a steady sufferer of both forms of attacks, I understand the mental, emotional, and physical toll it takes on a sufferer, as well as on the people in their support system. It's important to get a deep understanding of both forms of attacks, know how to deal with them, and teach a sufferer's support people what they can do to help. Here's what's going on in a person's inner world during an attack:

They begin sorting for danger

The person begins paying more attention to potential risks and less to potential safety. They do this by using focused "tunnel vision." For example, if someone is speaking to a group of 100 people, a person who's moving toward an attack will pick out the one angry-looking person in the crowd, bypassing the other 99 happy-looking people, and feel a sense of impending doom rise within them. A person who starts to experience stomach tightness might turn their attention to that and speculate about its cause rather than feeling out the comfort in their hands. This is clearly an unconscious intention to distort the outside information and sort for threats while simultaneously preparing the body for an impending attack.

Increasing the significance of the danger

The person feeling the rise of an attack begins unconsciously altering the sub-modalities (aspects of each sensory system) of their environment. All of a sudden, the size, distance, sounds, smells, etc., become distorted so that the threat seems greater than the resources within them to deal with it. As these sub-components of a person's sensory systems get altered, so does the way they think about the situation, which, in turn, creates an exaggerated emotional response to the situation.

Not being 'at cause'

The person begins growing the belief that these attacks "just happen," and are the result of things taking place on the outside. Little do they realize that there's an unconscious structure to panic attacks and a conscious structure to anxiety attacks since the emotions quickly overtake their reasoning capabilities. The attack is a result of their attention to representations of danger; it's rarely the result of the thing or situation itself.

The job of your subconscious mind is to take the pressure off of your conscious mind. The only problem with this is that the intense need for constant automation makes the system malfunction and go crazy, causing it to automate everything based on recordings it has taken around your life up until now. The road back to desensitization will undoubtedly take a level of understanding and courage to look into the eyes of uncertainty and to embrace it. A certain amount of inner dialogue representing evidence that supports the fact that panic in the moment doesn't have to lead to a general fearful overview of the world as a whole can help. But we don't want to strictly rely on logic to convince the subconscious mind and body, as there are more powerful ways to communicate than logic and evidence. As we move through this chapter, ask yourself which of the following three modes of stress you experience the most if attacks are a part of your current life experience.

3 modes of stress that accompany both anxiety and panic attacks

Fight – In fight mode, a person raises their voice, tension rises in their jaw and neck, they use strict and strong movements, show a high level of impatience, and their eyes lock onto a target or enemy, which results in a glazed look.

In fight mode, the intention is to take action in order to fight back against the thing that caused the experience in the first place. A person in fight mode looks for a fast solution to a challenge that may have been boiling to the surface for some time. Panic attacks are thought to be "out of the blue occurrences," while anxiety attacks are when the person knows the cause of the attack. These are important distinctions to make as we put the puzzle pieces of your attacks together. Although a panic attack feels out of the blue, a trail of cookie crumbs is always present. This means that the person has had needs that weren't met, emotions that have been repressed and fluctuating, thoughts that branched to other thoughts, and unconscious recognitions of fragments of previous experiences that get detected in the environment and cause the stress response.

For the sufferer in fight mode:

Don't try to get rid of the feelings and thoughts right away. Trying to push it away will only create more pressure, your expectations won't get met, and catastrophic thinking will be the result. Instead, let your body become less sensitized over time, when it believes it's the right time. The subconscious pairings related to fear get strengthened the harder we try to alter our state; we don't want that. This is where trust comes into play — to understand that the infinite intelligence within you will and always has come down from a panic or anxiety attack. The more you practice "Riding The Wave," the deeper those messages get sent, and the better chance that the next time you meet with the same external stimuli, the emotional reaction will shift.

These feelings are uncomfortable, not life-threatening. Remind yourself of this and act in line with adopting this new idea.

Your inner dialogue must transition from hardened ways of speaking to yourself to gentleness and full acceptance of what has occurred. Your system loves you unconditionally, and, in this moment, its goal is to protect you. So find the peace in that and begin responding with understanding as best you can.

For the supporter:

It's important that if you're a friend or family member of the person going through fight mode, you don't try to undermine their authority by interrupting them or questioning what they may be saying to you. You don't want to annoy them, and you certainly don't want to laugh at them.

Instead, you want to listen to them because it's important to understand that if a person can verbalize and say what's on their mind, in the way that they need to (emotionally), the experience won't become stored as a traumatic experience as much. The only way things get complicated in the future is if fighters repress what they're feeling; the symptoms related to that moment of repression can show up many years down the road. As a supporter, you want to offer solutions in the form of telling them the aspects of that experience they might not recognize. Their breathing may become shallow, but that's all it is; shallow, not life-threatening. They feel the need to be frantic, but it's just related to a stress response that misinterpreted the situation. These crucial pieces of information will begin to provide the sufferer with a broader viewpoint. This kind of calm recognition of what the sufferer is missing is gold since they will, in time, become the emotional state of the supporter. Remember, if the fighter doesn't have anything to fight against, they will begin easing off.

Flight – During the flight response, a person begins breathing very shallowly and sweating profusely. Their eyes are consistently looking away from what they were involved with before the attack, and their hands and feet are fiddling frantically. These signs are telltale signals that the reaction the person is feeling is to escape the situation now.

For the sufferer in flight mode:

In this mode of stress, you want to make sure you're not adding to the inner need to rush. Rushing will only strengthen the very thing you believe is a threat. Your system is telling you to escape because of an occurrence that has threatened your survival in some way, but you must do what you can to reinterpret the situation, and the main step is to bring your level of pace down by not rushing.

As you neutralize your speed — in walking, talking, and eventually breathing — you begin tapping into the middle ground between fast and slow. The more your internal focus turns to this middle ground, the deeper the signals will be sent to your nervous system to begin activating your parasympathetic rest-and-digest system. In future situations, your system will think twice before activating your stress response, as mental and emotional neutralness will appear. As your internal focus turns to the pace in how you go about the next little while, begin giving yourself a countdown before you head for the exit.

Begin counting from 60 down to 0 in a slow manner, and when you get to 0, only then will you allow yourself to escape the situation. Most likely, you'll begin opening yourself up to new perceptions, your symptoms will begin lessening, and your actions will respond to you staying where you are. The 60-second countdown begins to bring power back to the conscious mind. As the emotional state begins to shift, so will the voice within the conscious mind to help understand the situation better.

For the supporter – As the supporter for someone in flight mode, you want to make sure you don't shout at them as this can startle them while being in this sensitized place. Also, closed questions shouldn't be used (questions that lead to yes or no answers) since we want them engaged in the safety of the situation, and closed questions won't allow for access to their conscious, analytical mind as their speed slows down. It will only cause an increase in sensitivity. Give them open-ended questions to begin activating their pre-frontal cortex, showing them that they are open to choose, not their emotions. Humor is also a good option for supporters helping a sufferer in flight mode.

Freeze – Having worked with people over the years who come to me with anxiety disorders, there's always a common thread among them: many of them recall a moment of freezing in their childhood that led to subsequent moments of freezing, which only led to further sensitivity as time went on.

For the sufferer in freeze mode:

These people literally stopped moving (therefore stopping the arrival of oxygen to the lungs) as they felt a deep sense of helplessness in the situation. Their eyes glazed over, noticing nothing in particular, their bodies became droopy, and they showed a clear submissiveness in attitude. If in the present day, a sufferer is still experiencing a sense of freezing, I believe it's the most important stress response out of the three to disengage from. Simply because if a person fights back verbally or behaviorally, their system takes a certain amount of empowerment from the experience rather than storing it as a trauma. If a person leaves a situation (worst-case scenario), there's a sense of relief, and their conscious mind may become activated to the point that they go back in and alter their perceptions over the event.

If a person freezes beyond help for themselves, a picture is taken at the moment prior to the highest emotional intensity in that situation. This picture becomes stored in the brain — neural connections are formed and strengthened as to what's around the environment. It also gets stored in the body so that anything that even closely resembles the picture brings up emotions and physical sensations. Much of my work with others is applying different ways of reframing these moments of freezing so that they begin perceiving their entire childhood as less traumatizing. As well, methods that help speak to parts of the body that are still held captive from past trauma due to the freeze response can be very effective.

If you are experiencing a freeze response in the present moment, you want to make sure to remind yourself to breathe completely. Shallowness in the breath will only lead to further constriction in the body leading to further freezing and helplessness. In the present freeze mode, it's vital that you engage in a connection to your senses. The last thing we want is to fully succumb to these emotions so we actively look to engage in what we see (and possibly even see through what's happening that may be causing the distress), what we hear at that moment, what we feel against our physical bodies (our clothes, the wind, the sun, etc.), what we smell, and what we taste. Becoming active in your senses will help to disengage in the freeze response and re-engage with your sensory systems that are becoming negatively altered due to the strength of the emotions felt.

It's also very important to keep a dialogue going with whoever is with you. Work toward not bottling up the ideas and feelings, but expressing them fully and as clearly as possible to others.

For the supporter – Don't force the sufferer into any courageous act, don't try to snap them out of it or pump them up; it could lead to possibly retraumatizing the person and freezing even further. Instead, work on creating rapport with the sufferer without them recognizing what you're doing. This is done by matching their body language at that moment. If the sufferer sees this, they will understand that it's OK to come out of the freeze response gradually and that their safety person is truly here for them. Many times, when a supporter matches the posture, hand gestures, facial expressions, etc., of the sufferer, it creates the sense that they're not completely losing control and can, in time, regain control over their own systems.

Speak to the person slowly and softly. Since we now understand the power of speed, the supporter can communicate with the unconscious part of the sufferer to let them know (through the softness and slowness of their words) that this situation is a false alarm, and nothing more.

We must remember that the best way to end a panic attack or an anxiety attack is to recognize which unconscious or conscious patterns lead to the attack and keep it alive. In terms of a panic attack, it might be things like regret, unforgiveness, grief, anger, blame, or anything else that energetically grows stronger without awareness. In terms of an anxiety attack, the formula could be a situation from the past that hasn't been resolved and that the person knows about, but continues to play out — scenario after scenario — as to what might occur in the future because of what happened in the past.

Overcoming attacks requires a critical evaluation of yourself, something many people don't take the time to do, or say they don't know how. To accomplish this critical self-evaluation, carry an "emotions journal" and start writing down your emotional reactions throughout the day. It's not necessary to take note of your more neutral emotional states, but more so your extreme emotional states and what patterns of thoughts, speech, behaviors, or inner images may have led to that attack.

The best way to end panic and anxiety attacks is to prevent them from occurring in the first place, rather than waiting for the moment of panic to do something about it. Preparation doesn't create an environment for an attack to manifest; instead, it creates an environment to respond. If you and your support person aren't prepared for an attack, you will succumb to the emotional intensity of the moment. However, if you prepare, you'll be taking one more giant step in the direction of altering how you feel about your past, as well as the current situation.

General summary:

- Anxiety attacks have a conscious structure, a build-up to them.
- Panic attacks have an unconscious structure to them, as well.

- The sufferer must recognize these structures and begin recognizing how they may be misinterpreting things that are happening to them.
- Preparation and prevention is the best way to end anxiety and panic attacks, rather than look to counter them in the moment.
- Attacks come and go, they always have, and they always will; remember that the next time you're in the experience.

Summary for the support person:

- Practice patience during the attack that another person is experiencing. The sufferer will unconsciously mirror your emotional state more and more so you must communicate a sense of safety through your body language and words.
- Make sure not to go down the path of extremes. Meaning, projecting words like "you must stay" or "you must leave," for example. Challenge the perceptions of a sufferer, but don't force anything upon them.
- Remember that they are the only ones who can heal themselves. You are there to show a new perspective, remind them of the tools they must apply, and prepare them in case an attack occurs. But they must choose to walk this path wholeheartedly, and only them.
- Celebrate their wins with them. If they do a good job of countering an attack, remind them

of it later on and ask them about the lessons they may have learned.

- Take a look into their build-up toward an attack. Which thoughts, words, actions lead them closer and closer to an attack. They may not realize the formula that leads them to an attack, so your feedback here is valuable.

CHAPTER 17:

The Effects of People-Pleasing on Anxiety

"Stop pushing away who you truly want to become for the sake of pleasing others."

As a former people pleaser, I found myself a slave to the wants and needs of others, which resulted in heartache for me. The harder I would try, the more I expected of myself, and I literally rearranged my entire existence around what people wanted from me. I changed my vocabulary to match their crummy self-sabotaging words, only to meet with daily competitions on who had a tougher life. I altered the way I dressed to match their outfits so I wouldn't stick out in a crowd and also to have a chance of being more accepted. I kept quiet even though I had so much to add to conversations. I even took their verbal punishments, never sticking up for myself or rejecting their impressions of me. I would frequently wonder how I became so mentally frail — existing in the shadows of others but never truly making my mark or paving my own life path. Instead, my life was held together through the impressions of everyone I came in contact with. I felt less and less in power and gravitated more and more toward pleasing others.

We look to please others to gain acceptance and to feel a sense of significance in our lives since we felt so powerless as children

There are, of course, exceptions to this rule, but when you direct your focus to your younger years as a child, you'll notice plenty of insignificance and need for acceptance. What you did wasn't enough, nor was it good enough. Your parents and other teachers had great intentions for you, and the information they received from their authority figures simply got transferred to you. By people-pleasing today, we reconnect with our needs from childhood, at least a little bit, but that's better than nothing. Your boss, friends, and other family members start accepting you more, complimenting you more, and your people pleasing-behavior becomes habitual. You begin feeling at least a little sense of connection and significance, and there's no way you're going to let this go. Because if you stop people-pleasing and start prioritizing your well–being, you feel like you might lose this sense of significance and go back to being lost and feeling alone. We cling to what makes us feel good the fastest. If someone knows they will get a comforting response from someone by agreeing with them, that's what it'll be. Because to reject would be to also create conflict, and the last thing this person needs is to feel worse about themselves because they started something with someone. So they play it safe instead.

We look to please others because we're stuck in the system that tells us that our happiness is dependent on what others think about how we do things. This started the moment we came into this world, and it continued during our school years, into our adolescence, through college, into our adult work life, and so forth. It's a manipulative cycle because your worth isn't dependent on what others think of you; it's dependent on what you think of you. But try logically presenting that idea to your subconscious mind and you'll find total rejection of the new idea if you don't have a powerful enough toolbox for healing (responding skillsets). The habit of continually pleasing others takes you out of energetic alignment with all the good you desire in your life. You become more and more detached from seeing the big picture and the positive options on how to perceive everyday situations. You become handcuffed to making other people's goals come true while yours sit on the shelf with little to no growth. Pleasing others boosts our dopamine and serotonin levels, temporarily providing us with motivation and good feelings. The problem is that the bar gets raised daily, and we feel the need to do more and more for others as each day passes. This makes us feel more and more inferior because we find that we can't seem to meet the rising expectations of others.

Is this starting to sound familiar?

If so, just the simple recognition of these patterns should show you the direction your life is headed. You stay powerless in the face of everything and everyone until a time when you hit rock bottom and choose to direct your life rather than allow others to direct it. People-pleasing is different from connecting, although many can't see the difference in the moment. Connecting, on the other hand, emphasizes mutual respect between people, it doesn't mean both parties agree with each other on all levels, but it does mean we both take into consideration the thoughts, words, feelings, and actions of others. To look to please others constantly is the ultimate energy drainer there is. Yes, you can contribute positively to other people's lives, but you mustn't become a slave to the needs of everyone. As your self-confidence grows, you begin to feel more and more positive options in your mind starting to show up. You become liberated by this decision and these positive movements as you begin questioning the old you more and more.

Instead of looking to please others first, I want you to ask yourself, "What do I need right now?" Or, "What's best for my emotional health at this moment?" Remember, questions alone can open up new perceptions and actions in your life. These questions bring you back to the present (rather than the rewards you will attain from others by constantly pleasing them) and lessen the pressure that the world can put on you. Pleasing others means to neglect ourselves, and if we don't put ourselves first, we'll never be met with true happiness and true contribution to the betterment of this world. Without getting yourself "right," you will always be relying on other people and other things to do the work for you. Asking these types of questions come with answers like:

1) "I need to release what's on my mind to this person rather than suppress my thoughts and emotions. Because if I don't, I'll only be harming myself in the long run." Notice that the pleasure of holding in what you need to let out is now reversed, and pain takes its place as you put yourself first.

2) "I need to behave in such a way that gets my point across to people because if I don't, I'll pay the price by feeling like I should have acted differently later on in the day. This will negatively affect my sleep and keep me snowballing in the same direction tomorrow morning, and I can't have that anymore." By associating more and more pain to not doing something, we begin to tip the scales toward doing something different. Moving away from pain and toward pleasure is the ultimate motivator a person needs to ponder in order to make positive changes in their life.

3) "I need to stop agreeing with everything my family says because if I don't, I'll just turn out more like them, and this will affect my children." Another powerful example of pain and pleasure. Pain to following the status quo, which then will affect the person's children negatively, and pleasure to changing for the sake of giving the person's children a more positive and pleasant life on their own terms.

It's rare to meet someone who hasn't been affected by people-pleasing at some point in their lives. The habit of people-pleasing soon becomes an indicator of social anxiety. Many people mistake social anxiety as only being extremely shy; this is completely false. Socially anxious people who are constantly seeking approval from others by being excessively complimentary and overly generous turn themselves over to a type of social anxiety. Let's remember that social anxiety is about being evaluated and judged by others, which then leads to the need for external validation. Some people avoid this through people-pleasing and others by extreme levels of avoidance. Since avoidance brings up less inner strain and pressure, it's the go-to response for many social anxiety sufferers. Here are some other things to make sure you're aware of:

Buying people's affection

What's the fastest way to get someone to feel good about themselves, and you? Buy them something. There's only one realization you must come to, though, and that is that real friends will never need anything from you but your simple presence.

Say 'NO' more!

To put people-pleasing before your happiness is just not right. Ask yourself right now if you have a hard time saying no to people, and if there are any people in your life right now who might be taking advantage of this. Learning to say no opens up more time for you and prioritizes your needs before other people's needs. The initial discomfort of saying no will be followed by a deep sense of empowerment and self-respect.

Care less about other people's opinions

The cheapest and most common thing in the world is an opinion. These days people don't really listen; they just wait their turn to talk, and they can't wait to pick out your mistakes in the hope of strengthening their ego. People's negative opinions of you are a reflection of deep-seated unresolved emotions and experiences in their lives. It has very little, or nothing, to do with you and everything to do with their repressed rage that found a small opportunity to discharge temporarily.

The great football player Cristiano Ronaldo once played for a small Portuguese club named Sporting Lisbon before receiving a request by one of the biggest football clubs in the world — Manchester United. As the decision to go or stay weighed on young Ronaldo's mind, he remembers his agent giving him some wise advice to make sure he was prepared should he choose to go to this huge club. He said, "It's not that you have to be concerned about the level of play; it's that you have to make sure you are ready for backlash by the fans, the media, teammates, your manager, and just about everyone no matter what you do there." If Ronaldo took this transfer on, he would have had to agree never to allow the opinions of others to affect him on and off the football pitch. He did accept the offer and went on to become a great champion. This is the same opportunity you have at this moment: to level up in your personal life and care less around what other people think will come with dirty looks, disagreements, dislike, and much more from people you know and don't know. The question is, are you ready? If the answer is yes, you begin setting the terms for your life, and if the fear is too great, you will live a comfortable life people-pleasing and never truly find out what you're capable of emotionally and behaviorally. Choose now.

We live in a world where society punishes people who are real, and praises people who are fake

But let me tell you something, I have a handful of trustworthy, intelligent and fun-loving friends who I have a great connection with and that's enough for me. Social media today makes us believe that the more friends and followers we have online, the happier and more successful we are. What garbage. Behind the blissfully fake selfies that most influencers take today on Instagram is a lonely, unfulfilled soul looking for truth, but only finding more drama. Being a slave to the number of followers and friends you have online converts offline as well. There always seems to be a void that needs to be filled. That void can't be filled by anyone else but you, but it's you who needs to come to terms with this sooner rather than later. It's also time for you to make your own decisions rather than waiting your turn to follow someone else. Following the lead of others can seem like the easier route, because of habit, and it makes you feel connected and less lonely, but you've mixed up loneliness with inner peace. You think spending time alone is harmful when, in fact, it's the best time to get to know yourself better. These are the types of perceptions that need shifting. People-pleasing becomes social slavery. Loneliness isn't boredom; it's personal time. And saying no doesn't make you a bad person; it keeps the power in your relationships balanced at 50/50.

Stop telling people that 'everything is fine' when it's not

Honestly, it's time to tell the truth: The healthiest people are expressive when they need to be, and internal when they need to be. If there's something between you and another person that you want to discuss, go ahead and say it. That way, you can stop beating yourself up on the inside by stuffing it deeper and deeper down. Your ego mind always makes future events worse than what they'll be and also much better than what they'll be. It thrives on extremes. So what you think will be a disastrous event, if you express what you truly think will most likely be met with deep understanding by the other person. Not only this, mutual respect will begin forming since best friends are the ones who tell it to you like it is. So sacrifice a moment of discomfort, share your true feelings, and grow as a person now.

Summary:

- Life in all aspects gets better when we express what we truly need to express to others.
- People-pleasing is a habit that mustn't go unrecognized any longer; it must be brought to your attention and connected to the pain that it brings with it.
- Connecting to all the pleasurable outcomes once the habit of people-pleasing is over and done with will create an emotional movement within you that will get you to take steady action. Remember, pain to staying with what you're doing and pleasure to changing.
- Having self-love and self-respect isn't arrogance; it's placing priority back onto yourself since nothing you do will have any lasting positive effect if you don't prioritize your overall well-being first.
- Saying no isn't a bad thing; it's a great thing! The road to ending the destructive habit of people-pleasing starts with the word no.

CHAPTER 18:

Meditation For Healing Anxiety

"It's the fear of stillness that causes so much useless action in people's lives today."

Meditation has been a tricky topic in the anxiety world as of late for many different reasons. Coming straight from the perspectives of many of the anxiety sufferers I've been in contact with over the years, here are a few questions I hear consistently:

What is meditation good for?
How long does it take to see results?
What if I can't meditate for long periods of time?
Do you have to be spiritual to do meditation?
What are the best types of meditations for anxiety?

There are many more questions, of course, so leaving meditation out of this book made no sense to me. A friend of mine introduced me to meditation during the 6th year of my 6-year struggle with an anxiety disorder. At the beginning, I remember talking myself out of doing it, as well as having my unconscious not allow me to sit still for any period of time. With a system so invested in the lurking threat right around the corner, the last thing it wants you to do is to have you close your eyes, consciously breathe, and stay still. That would be like allowing the saber-toothed tiger to walk around you before being eaten up. You can see how this is a typical evolutionary response to daily life that our ancestors went through.

I remember thinking that the only time I had ever stopped completely and not fully engaged in something was when I was asleep. It was a strange realization. Here's a person introduced to a tool that would benefit them deeply and I had never experienced anything close to it. To make peace with peace wasn't easy at the beginning, so I stopped doing it instead. But then I began thinking that if I stop doing everything I think might contribute to my anxiety recovery over time, I'll be a hermit stuck in my bedroom for life. I had to give meditation a shot, and I needed to commit to proving to myself that I could do what I thought I couldn't.

At first, I struggled to get any momentum during meditation, and I found it quite silly. "Shouldn't I be doing something instead of wasting my time just sitting here?" I thought. It was obvious that my brain had paired up "me time" and slowing things down to being unproductive, greedy, and even lazy.

The other problem I ran into was that I began with the mindset that meditation was going to heal my anxiety. That's a lot of pressure on meditation. I realized that this mindset needed to change since the roots of my anxiety were in my childhood due to freezing helplessly in situations where my entire system became overwhelmed. These moments froze the experience in time in my body and my brain, causing my perceptions to become distorted and to think of myself in very negative ways.

The proper mindset toward meditation is that it's a tool to help you uncover the roots of your anxiety and the missing pieces of information. It also helps to calm your nervous system. Meditation is a connection to an inner intelligence within you called the superconscious mind, which is responsible for the miracles in life as well as deeper wisdom. It doesn't heal your anxiety disorder; it provides the clarity that will help you to begin seeing things differently, as well as provide a break for your overactive, adrenaline-fueled body.

Clarity is the goal for all methods used today to heal anxiety disorders. It's the moments throughout the day that come to our conscious awareness that help us see things in a different light that provide the changes in the brain and body. These moments are gold. The only problem is that the hard-wired, "tired but wired" system is constantly at play within an anxiety sufferer, so they rarely spend any time on the clarity that comes to them. Instead, they move right back into worry and looking for the catastrophic possibilities in the next life situation.

Whenever I'm asked which habits have benefited me the most in my life to overcome emotional distress, I always say reframing, responding, and, of course, meditation. Meditation has allowed me to believe in the possibility of becoming a new me. Meditation practices don't insist that you become a Tibetan monk and travel off to caves in faraway mountaintops. Anyone of any spiritual or religious background can apply meditation and gain the benefits from it.

For meditation practices to be useful to the anxiety sufferer, we must make sure we understand a few key principles:

Focus on quality over quantity

I remember gaining tremendous benefit from meditation by doing 1-minute sessions twice a day. Most people would say that sounds pointless and won't provide much benefit. But the truth is that this practice is meant to strengthen your focus, something anxiety sufferers lost many years ago. Their focus is regularly turned directly to the worst possible scenario, and no matter what takes place in their outer world, they can't seem to focus on one thing at a time. Instead, they are distracted and reactive to anything and everything. Daily meditation will help put power back into your conscious mind. The key is to remember that it's not the length of time you spend but rather the quality of the session. It's a tremendous win in my opinion when a severe-level anxiety sufferer can sit in silence, focusing on their in-breath and out-breath with their eyes closed for 1 minute (more techniques later). So don't ever get caught up in how long, but how focused and absorbed you are instead.

Eliminate expectations

Too many people attempt a meditation session with the hope of putting 30 years of emotional traumas behind them for good. Let's get real; the chances of that happening are slim to none. Meditation practices are for allowing changes to happen when they do, not forcing them to happen. Also, if there are too many expectations behind your practice, you will find yourself too hyperaroused to let go enough to focus on what you need to. Allow change to happen as it does during meditation and set your high expectations aside.

Keep it simple

These days, meditation practices are getting more and more complicated, with so many people looking to bring the next big thing into the world. The power of meditation is in its simplicity, and we mustn't make it more complicated than what it needs to be. All that's required is sitting upright or lying down in an environment where you won't be distracted, and allowing your focus to turn to your in-breath and out-breath in a long, rhythmic fashion. Breathing through your diaphragm is an important part of meditation as you strengthen your focus and lower your stress levels with each long breath.

As the world gets more and more complicated and frantic, we must counter these energies with lighthearted daily meditation. It's a staple in my daily life, and I have been doing the same three meditations now for the past 8 years. It can become a part of your daily routine as long as you get your priorities right. To gain as much as you can from meditation, begin with the mindset that you come first, and that your well-being affects everyone else's.

At its essence, meditation is mindfulness; you must allow yourself to be in the moment and bring your focus back when it wants to move onto something else. People today are becoming more and more hijacked by their worries and memories, especially in the case of recovery from trauma. Mindfulness is an essential part of healing that strengthens your calm awareness and allows you to detach from your limiting thoughts quickly. It can help bring you back to the true possibility of a future situation rather than an imagined catastrophic one. This was an important recognition during my healing journey; I began caring less and less about anything that brought on anxiety.

I asked myself what the worst thing that could happen was. The answer was, I'd die. OK, I started thinking, if it happens, I get to experience a whole new state of consciousness. If I die, yes, I'll have to depart from what I know in this current lifetime, but I mustn't fight with the cycle of life and instead embrace it. My new belief was that even if the worst thing happens, I'll still be fine, and meditation was a big factor in making this belief real in my heart.

When you conquer the fear of dying, that's when you're truly free

It's the hardest thing any of us is called to do since there's a tremendous amount of uncertainty to it. But it's a necessary thing we must take the time to understand and place a new meaning over.

Some of the benefits to a daily meditation practice are:

- Increased immune function
- Decreased inflammation at a cellular level
- Decreased pain
- Increased positive emotion; makes you feel positively connected to the world

- Decreased depression
- Increased compassion
- Increased focus and attention; improves your ability to multitask
- Improved memory

Some of the myths about meditation are:

- You need to wear a robe
- You must sit in a lotus position
- You must clear your mind to be able to meditate (in the beginning, this won't be the case at all)
- Meditation is just New Age nonsense
- Meditation involves joining a cult
- Meditation is just for relaxation
- Meditation takes hours to benefit from
- Books are the way to learn meditation
- Meditation is hard work

Meditation is the practice of learning how to pay attention. When we take the clarity gained from meditation, we can apply it toward observing the world without judgment, rather than experiencing neutral situations and making them worse. What's necessary for anxiety sufferers, no matter what the specific challenge, is to learn how to strengthen their curiosity. As we become more curious and less reactive, we begin to understand why our bodies react in such nervous ways to meeting a stranger, getting up in the morning, bodily sensations, or anything else. Curiosity helps to put the puzzle pieces to your anxiousness together, creating a disassociated (detached) state over an associated (fully attached) state.

Soon you begin looking at your inner distress or external threats as if you're watching them on a movie screen rather than being in the movie and being watched. I now understand this to be a vital human trait to living a long and prosperous life. Since everyone I know over the age of 85 who still has the vibrant energy of a 35-year-old, is curious about everything.

Here are the three main meditations I recommend for anxiety sufferers looking to begin or maintain their current practice:

Color meditation

Since the first language we learned when we came out of the womb was color (some colors were connected to safety, some to threat), we can utilize this language to bring about fast changes in how we feel. Color meditation is simple, as are all my recommended meditation practices, but don't be fooled; I believe the simplest meditations, when mastered, become life-altering.

Here are the steps:

- Sit or lie in a comfortable position and close your eyes.
- Locate the part of your body where you're holding emotional distress.
- Locate the color associated with that feeling (many times red or black).
- Find out what the safest color is that comes to mind for you; a comforting, trusting,

empowering color (go with your first impression).

- Begin with a full out-breath of the distressing color, and begin breathing in your safety color to the part of your body where you were holding the distress.
- Continue breathing out the color of distress.
- Continue breathing in your safety color and breathing out your distress color for as long as needed.

Color, sound, and vibration are our earliest known ways of understanding things when we came to this world. This means that the nervous system gets what you're doing much more than your conscious mind. To your conscious mind, it's just any other color (remember that this mind wasn't developed until around the age of 5), but to your subconscious mind, it has been pairing up colors, sounds, and vibrations to safety and threat since the moment you were born. As you get more and more comfortable with color meditation, you'll begin allowing your safety color to move throughout your whole body. This brings an overall sense of comfort to most people, a feeling of being loved and held. After a few highly focused color meditation sessions, notice how you begin responding differently to things in the outside world.

Mantra meditation

My version of mantra meditation places emphasis on a safety word (or two words, maximum). This safety word stays on repeat until the mind turns to the past and future (and it will) before refocusing back on the safety word again. Throughout ancient history, healers in all tribes and past civilizations placed great emphasis on affirmations done with a certain level of rhythm. A good example of this is within Shamanism, where a drum beat — accompanied by a phrase or a multitude of phrases — begins to impact the sufferer in ways that creates shifts physiologically. As their brainwave patterns begin slowing down, the mantra becomes absorbed within the subconscious mind and body more readily as the protector of false beliefs (the critical factor) goes out for a metaphorical lunch break. The mantra can be repeated on the inside or the out loud; I prefer on the inside, as it helps me concentrate even more.

The steps for mantra meditation are as follows:

1) Sit or lie down in a comfortable position and close your eyes.
2) Intuitively feel the positive impact of one particular word that comes to mind (I use the words heal, truth, free, calm, and power).
3) Take a deep breath in and, as you breathe out, fully repeat this word to yourself on the out-breath.
4) Allow yourself to feel the emotional and bodily effects of this word with each turn.
5) Keep going until your desired time is reached.

I like to repeat my power word right at the moment of my out-breath and finish it way before my out-breath is completed. Some people like to drag it along throughout the entire out-breath. It doesn't matter; be playful, be curious, and go with what works best for you.

Focus meditation

Focus meditation places emphasis on three of your five main senses. When I ask many of my clients what they want to accomplish within a set period of working with me, many of them say, "I just want to be more involved." This means they want to feel connected to what they're doing and the people around them rather than being overly internal and sensitized. What focus meditation does is take you out of reacting unconsciously and put you back into all the things in your external world that you're missing.

Here are the steps:

1) Sit or lie down in a comfortable position.
2) Begin breathing slowly and deeply.
3) In your internal world (your mind's eye/imagination), bring up a peaceful environment that makes you feel calm and centered.
4) Visually: Notice what you see in a broad sense (many different things), followed by noticing one calming thing, in particular, you see (narrow focus).
5) Auditory: Notice all the things you hear in that picture (broad), followed by focusing on just one thing you hear that creates a sense of inner peace within (narrow focus).
6) Kinesthetic: Notice all the things you feel against your physical body (broad focus) — the clothes you're wearing, the wind against your face, the sun on your body, rocks below your feet, etc. — followed by narrowing your focus onto one thing you feel against your physical body.
7) When you've taken an even amount of time between broad and narrow for all three senses,

just allow yourself to be for a few moments in that environment without focusing on anything in particular before opening your eyes.

The ability to build the skill of going from broad to narrow perspectives gives a person tremendous focusing power as they go about their day. In time, they'll feel like they can bring themselves away from distress or over-focusing on all the things that could go wrong to focusing on all the things that could go right. Focus meditation is loved by many of my clients because they feel like it returns power to them, rather than succumbing to "negative" emotions. They start to feel like they can control what they have control over, and that is a huge win for any anxiety sufferer.

Many people have a misconception that becoming anxiety free will ultimately lead to some kind of huge celebration

The truth of the process is that freedom is not necessarily exciting but, in fact, a very peaceful and quiet transition. If the mind can't quiet itself, and if thoughts can't be attuned to being like clouds that come and go, there will be no freedom; it simply can't be with so much internal chatter going on. A sense of wonder begins to show up within a person through the process of meditation and anxiety recovery, almost like "what's next?" A sense of total capability and a feeling of breaking down the limiting inner walls start to appear. In the words of the spiritual guru Osho:

Meditation is a quality of being that you bring to the act. It is not a particular act, it is not that you do this then it is meditation – that you sit in a certain posture, and you keep your spine erect, and you keep your eyes closed or you look at the tip of your nose or you watch your breath, then it is meditation. No, these are just devices for the beginners.

He continues with,

Do you know that the words meditation and medicine come from the same root? Meditation is a kind of medicine; its use is only for the time being. Once you have learned the quality, then you need not do any particular meditation, then the meditation has spread all over your life. Only when you are meditative 24 hours a day then can you attain, then you have attained. Even sleeping is meditation.

There are a few things to unpack within the words of Osho. First, that meditation is a way of life, not any particular technique. The beginning stages of meditation are guided and slightly mechanical, but, in time, meditation occurs while you walk, converse with others, sit, eat, read, etc. A person begins feeling like they are in a state of meditation all day every day; I believe this is true enlightenment, a non-forceful acceptance of inner peace no matter what. And you will get there.

Summary:

- Meditation is a tool to open up the mind of the anxiety sufferer further to begin seeing through the habits that cause them distress. It provides shifts in perception as well as physiological changes that further help to cement the person's new direction, and new identity.
- Simple is always better.

- The quality of the meditation practice is more important than the quantity. A few minutes daily within a meditative state with full absorption is much more powerful than 30 minutes of distracted and pessimistic detachment.
- Meditation practices begin turning into a daily way of being. It begins affecting all aspects of your life and brings you toward unconditional love for yourself and all things.
- Mediation is not a fad; it's a way of life.

CHAPTER 19:

Resistance To Change

*"It's not about managing anxiety;
it's about developing a new you."*

In the past, have you ever felt like no matter what you do, you never seem to be able to maintain your good progress over anxiety? It always seems like something is pulling you back, not allowing you to fully change certain aspects of yourself, like your thinking, feeling, and imagery. I was in this situation for a long time, going in and out of different emotions, thinking, in the back of my mind, I'd always have some degree of anxiety. There are three very important reasons for this resistance, and they're all connected to your survival. Let's explore them:

Anything that goes against what you believe to be true

The first factor in resistance to change is one that's related to your core beliefs. Anything that's true for you, you will sort for and look to justify even if it harms you. The brain likes to work efficiently with as little interference from the neocortex (thinking brain) as possible. Less thinking means fewer new lessons to learn, and less energy spent. This is a massive roadblock for many anxiety sufferers determined to free themselves, and it must be understood if we want to change it.

Just because something is better for you doesn't mean the mind, body, and spirit will accept it. The earliest experiences and continued repetition play the leading role in deciding which beliefs get stronger and which ones don't make it to the party. What's true in your life right now could be any or all of the following beliefs:

- I'm slow at learning new skills.
- I'm socially awkward and people don't like me.
- My only safety place is my home.
- Large groups of people are intimidating.
- My symptoms could very well mean I've already caught a life-threatening disease.

If an idea shows up that opposes these well-trained core beliefs, it has very little chance of moving from an idea to a belief. Safety is dependent on what's familiar. Even though when you objectively take a good hard look at each of the examples above or any other limiting beliefs you have, they're very much false in every way. You're actually quite fast at learning new skills; if you apply the right formula, you can make anywhere your safe place, and your symptoms are most likely a result of an external trigger that went unrecognized by your conscious awareness.

Say this idea to yourself right now:

"I make $1 million a year!"

Give it a moment and then notice what happened.

Most likely, you had an elated feeling like "that would be pretty cool" (if you don't have that kind of income already) followed by the reasons why you'll never attain it. The conscious mind liked the idea, but the core beliefs kicked in soon after, which then leads to going back to life as it always was; in this, case irrationally fearful. This is the usual cycle for any new ideas. If only the first conscious idea were focused on for longer and connected to branches of other ideas (spiderweb effect), it would lead to sustaining the original emotion that showed up as a result of liking the idea. Where our focus goes is what becomes real in our mind and body. If we want to overcome anxiety, we have to retrain our focus alongside all the other things that used to give us good feelings, like smiling, laughing, and bodily contact.

People who can utilize the vital skill of responding over reacting unconsciously to everyday situations usually have had a less traumatic childhood than others, and have had more balance in their mind between ideas. They can more easily adopt a newer idea because the fearful, irrational thoughts haven't been so engrained at a belief level. Should more time pass and they find themselves falling into the snowball effect more and more (a build-up of negativity, pessimism, and doubt), they will also have a more difficult time turning it all around.

Let me emphasize again, though, the timeline for healing differs from one person to the next, and comes down to too many factors, such as environment, skillsets, mindset, social circle, hunger levels, tiredness levels, and more. So, keep in mind that if you follow your deeper intuition and do what you know is right for you, alongside consistently responding and reframing through the teachings behind RIC, positive changes are inevitable.

Anything that goes against how we think others will see us

It's unfortunate, but this might be the biggest roadblock of them all to healing anxiety. Believe it or not, your well-intended family, friends, and, heck, even acquaintances, have an impact on your healing. Whether your anxiety has gone noticed or unnoticed by them, you will unconsciously (sometimes even consciously) reject positive change to maintain the status quo. Why would you change a good thing, right? Your social circle is growing and the majority of your family are worrywarts. Imagine how uncomfortable you would be at the dinner table talking about your progress while everyone else is competing to see who had the worst day? Yes, you'd be highly uncomfortable before tucking your tail between your legs and going right back to matching their words and emotional states. Then a few days go by, and you're super motivated thanks to all those motivational videos on YouTube (don't even get me started on those), and you say enough is enough, today is the day I change! You start with an excellent outcome-focused approach to your morning only to hit that 2 p.m. wall because you've motivated yourself into physical depletion. As you have lunch with your co-workers, you go right back to the way they know you the best — anxiety.

Instead of sacrificing a few people in their lives, some sufferers would rather take their anxiety to the grave. They don't want to change too much or step on people's toes because of the risk of being ridiculed for their change work. Many times, that's the energy you receive from those walking zombies you call friends and close family. The unconscious message they're sending is, "if you change and leave us behind, you're no longer in our social circle." Oh, and good luck trying to bring them on board with you to heal their own locked-up emotions, repressions, and identity issues; most of them won't budge.

I know I sound quite pessimistic here, but it's the truth! And if I don't bring this into your awareness, you'll end up wondering why change is so hard. No one is fully ready to heal until they are ready to sacrifice the people in their lives that they believe will reject their healing. Don't get me wrong when I mean sacrifice. I don't mean telling dad to screw off because Dennis said your father is responsible for the roots of your resistance. Sacrifice, in this context, means to temporarily not partake in usual dialogues, avoidances or limiting behaviors, certain environments, and other negative habits you have built up with others. It's your choice to either let them know what's going to take place for the next little while and who you're turning into and filling them in on whether they'd like to live this inspiring transition with you, or not.

Anything that goes against how you see yourself

How you view yourself will affect the way you perceive things as well as your actions. Everyone has a label that they walk around with that sits more at an unconscious level than it does at a conscious level. Here are a few general labels people walk around with each day:

- Worrywart
- Social butterfly
- The Rock
- Unworthy of all
- Mr. or Mrs. Struggles
- The Fighter
- Mr. Cool

As you can see, some of these labels are on the positive end and some on the negative. They are no accident and have manifested over time to become who you think you are. A good example of how my negative label affected me went something like this:

I am Mr. Struggles, and life is hard. I have to fight for everything or else I don't deserve having anything. I must live with a certain degree of punishment each day or else I don't feel like myself. When unanticipated challenges show up in my life, I berate myself for experiencing them and try to avoid them at all costs. I am Mr. Struggles.

Imagine living in that mind and body daily, yuck. You can see how my past self-label of Mr. Struggles kept me within a certain comfort zone. The good that came my way didn't fit with Mr. Struggles, so anytime I heard a compliment from someone, for example, on some inner progress, I would quickly turn the focus of the conversation back onto them out of sheer discomfort. Do you do this? Step one is admitting who you artificially believe you are.

The resistance here can come from an action you're forced to make, a comment by someone else, a positive idea that flashed in your mind, an image of optimism for the future, anything. Someone with a negative perspective of themselves will spend very little time building on anything different; in this case, optimistic outcomes. You see this form of resistance each and every day because the majority of the world lives in a state of comfortable suffering. This way, they know what's to come and won't be surprised by any changes to how they feel. Can you see how backward all of this is? Can you see how limited your life has become due to habit? My goal here is to turn you toward what's possible, and in order for you to start seeing what's possible for you and your life, you must make a conscious choice to see past the limits you've placed on yourself.

When the universe shows you a different side of you, it's your job to explore it, not reject it. If you explore the new, you're stepping out of the comfortable suffering zone and into the learning zone. Within that learning zone, just outside your comfort zone, you begin understanding the truth of who you are and what you're capable of. The learning zone must be met with each day without expectation of what's to come. This is when a reconnection shows up between you and God. This is when more and more questioning shows up over what you've believed is true over the years, and you begin leveling up your identity.

As a new label within shows up, you begin sensing a newfound excitement come into your life. Life is worth living again, one day doesn't match the last, and you begin gravitating to like-minded people. This is possible for anyone, so keep up the learning, understanding, and applying from this book, warrior.

Summary:

- You might not recognize the forms of resistance that show up because your subconscious mind can regard attempts to cleanse it from negative beliefs as a threat, and can create obstacles of "protection" against your efforts toward change. Now that you have more awareness about resistance, the question is, what are you going to do about it?

- Life is to be lived outside your comfort zone, within the learning zone each day in order for more self-love and compassion to show up.

- One person or an entire armies' opinion of you doesn't have to be a part of your inner label/identity. You choose who you become; no one else has that power from this point forward.

- Questioning your pessimistic and catastrophic ideas may go against the family or friend dynamic you may be sharing, and this is a sacrifice you must make to create positive change.

- Your outer results are an expression of your personal label; choose wisely if you want things to improve, and stay relentless in becoming that person in each situation you face. In fact, one of the best questions you can repeatedly ask yourself throughout the day is, "Am I in alignment with my new identity?" If the answer is yes, keep doing what you're doing; if the answer is no, change something right then and there.

CHAPTER 20:

Responding: Your Toolbox for Healing

*"The fear of things going wrong is never
the way to make things go right."*

Responding originated within Stoicism, an ancient Greek school of Philosophy that recognized that certain destructive emotions resulted from errors in perception and judgment. Stoicism taught how to minimize a person's negative emotions and maximize their joy and gratitude. CBT (cognitive behavioral therapy) is the modernized Stoicism in that it helps people alter their unhelpful behaviors and re-perceive their cognitive distortions. Stoicism and CBT help to strengthen the resourcefulness of the conscious mind so that in time, a new habit can be built over the old cognitive and behavioral habits that don't fulfill a person's desires.

Responding, as described in this book, is along the lines of these methods and philosophies. Over the years, I've taught responding to many people who have seen a tremendous change in their emotional state. In this chapter, I'll reveal to you powerful skillsets that you can bring with you in your TFH (toolbox for healing) to counter any intrusive thoughts, icky feelings, or other unhelpful experiences.

Responding can undoubtedly be used at any time of the day; however, we want to focus more on the first 10 seconds right after a distressing thought or feeling arises. This is when a counter must take place in order to guide us toward safety and neutralness, rather than irrational thinking and franticness.

Responding is an acronym for:

R – **Reply** to the idea
E – Be **effective**
S – **Strengthen** the new interpretation
P – Head in a **positive** direction
O – **Own** the new response
N – Question **negatives**
D – **Direct** consciously

It's very common, in the anxiety world, to hear the word "acceptance" being tossed around. Acceptance, in this context, means to accept whatever fear or negative idea comes into your mind, along with any unhelpful feelings, or physical symptoms. I used to be a big fan of acceptance until a few years ago when I noticed more and more people having trouble with this response to their irrational fears. It's kind of like having a pink elephant in your living room and trying to ignore it; it's pretty much impossible. So, behind acceptance, there must be a certain skillset that eventually leads to acceptance. This route has much more potential for success than passively accepting the negatives.

Responding comes in three categories. Within a week of familiarizing yourself with all three categories, you'll begin intuitively knowing which skillset to use for whatever situation you encounter. This is a massive part of the RIC teachings — to trust your intuition in the moments of distress, knowing you have within you all the answers you need for any situation.

The three categories are:

Cognitive – This is your ability to counter one idea with another in a way that begins turning the feelings in your body around, and changes where your focus goes. Cognitive responding strengthens the new beliefs you want to engrain in your subconscious to make it habitual and automatic, in time. Cognitive responding doesn't mean creating a dialogue between your irrational and rational choices; it means setting a targeted, new viewpoint over the situation.

Physiological – Physiological responding means to work with your body in ways that send clear signals of safety to your nervous system. The safer your nervous system feels in any given situation, the quicker the pairings in your mind will change from an external stimuli being a threat to it being harmless.

Auditory – Auditory responding means to listen to the voice in your head in a way that lessens the potential of those intrusive thoughts happening. Many times we "listen" our way into negative feelings as the thoughts in our head get louder, more direct, closer, or even come with scary pictures. In my experience working with people, I've found that this form of responding works fast and consistently, no matter what the problem is.

To use these three categories and the skills within them effectively, we have to know what our short-term goal is. We need to know when they are working and if we need to implement them differently, or more consistently, to get the desired result. Our overall goal is to change the way we feel in anxious moments, of course, but our short-term goal is to create disinterest around the thoughts or feelings in the body, and boredom toward them.

When disinterest and boredom show up, the anxious thought no longer holds any power over you

When this happens, we can begin becoming more absorbed in what's going on in our outside world — with our work, playing with our kids, tasting the food we're eating, being one with the conversation we're in, and so forth.

What's important is to give you something you can use, and use now. For me, if something doesn't work quickly and efficiently, I don't recommend it. Why give someone a coping strategy and tell them that anxiety will have to be lived with for the rest of their life when it's not even true? F**k coping! Just look around you and notice how many anxiety success stories there are; there are tons! But they don't make the front-page news, or a highly ranked blog these days. Those pages are reserved for fear and pain, since that's what speaks to the survival part of the brain the fastest.

Now, let's get your daily toolbox for healing ready.

Cognitive Responding

Cognitive responding is like redirecting the mind. It's like walking down one street for however long you've been suffering from anxiety, and then suddenly making a sharp turn down an unfamiliar street. Obviously, your mind wants to stay on the street it's most familiar with, but we all know where that leads to, right? Inner pain! So enough of that. There are literally hundreds, if not thousands, of cognitive skillsets out there that get tossed around from one CBT-based book to another, and from one therapist to the next. But I've developed a few that I've found meet the goals of disinterest and boredom the fastest. They are:

Snap, catch!

All you'll need for this cognitive response is an elastic band. Here are the steps for Snap, Catch:

- Snap your elastic band on your wrist the moment you feel you've engaged with the negative thought or feeling in your body. This will help to **catch the thought in action and break the negative pattern** that may be developing.
- **Challenge the negative idea by asking yourself questions** like, "How many times has this idea actually happened?" Or, "Have I actually seen anyone else in-person experience this?" Or "Is this an idea that is truly mine, or is it my mom's, dad's, or someone else's?" As you can see, step two is all about challenging the idea with questions, and how much evidence it actually holds.
- **Replace the idea with a new one and build it up with further evidence**. As you replace the idea

with a new, more optimistic future outcome, you also add evidence behind it like this: "This physical symptom of anxiety is due to the meeting I have coming up. It's not a sign of a physical problem since this happens often." Or, "I can face the day ahead, and I look forward to facing the day ahead because I'm in a transition from where I was to who I'm becoming." Or "In this social gathering, people are more interested in themselves than they are in what I might say or do that's embarrassing. I've said and done many embarrassing things in my past and people still like me."

The Snap, Catch response emphasizes catching the thought in action — before the spiderweb effect takes place (creating deeper emotions) — as well as building evidence of both its limited possibility and the new, more-likely outcome. I used an elastic band every day for 3 months during my healing from anxiety, and I can tell you it was my best friend after a while. When choosing your elastic band, look for one that has a bright color and is thick enough to grab your attention. The last thing you want is a regular, thin brown elastic band; that won't remind you to Snap, Catch, challenge, and replace negative thoughts when they arise.

As you practice this method more and more consistently, you won't even need the elastic band anymore. You'll begin to feel boredom and disinterest when any catastrophic idea shows up, and a positive habit will take over. Remember, if you're engaged enough in this response, you won't have to do it many times each day. We don't want your wrist turning purple; we want absorption and to meet our goal of disinterest and boredom as quickly as possible. So focus is key. The emotional shift is what will bring about the desired outcome.

Diving deeper!

I love diving deeper because it turns you into a mental detective. Through this skillset, you'll be asking yourself one powerful question to spur on a wave of doubt behind the negative idea and momentum toward a new one. The question you will ask yourself is:

"What Else Could This Mean?"

Here's a real-world example:

You wake up in the morning and realize that you didn't sleep as well as you wanted to. You're feeling tired and groggy. The easy thing to do is to listen to the negative ideas in your head that tell you today's going to be awful, you might get fired, or your health is declining.

So you ask yourself, "What else could this mean?"

As you dive deeper, you respond to yourself with thoughts like, "This means that I'll just have to be more compassionate toward myself today," or "This means that I'll have to take on less and ask for more help from others today," or "This means that I'll need to spend more time in nature today to recharge."

You can see how the quality of our questions can dictate the quality of our emotions. Ask yourself a better question and your entire day can completely change. Again, our goal for all responding skillsets is practicality. Can we use it right here and now? The answer here is yes. From here on, keep building up the evidence that favors the new response. More evidence and more facts that support the answer to "What else could this mean?" means the faster we'll get to boredom and disinterest over the old, limiting thought.

The Power of 'Or'!

Anxiety sufferers habitually fall for the worst possible outcome. That is until they can begin using the word "or," which is a powerful internal (or external, if you choose to say it out loud) response to an anxiety-provoking idea that has the potential to shift your focus to a more likely outcome instantly. Here's an example:

You're watching your child play on the playground. The thought arises, "What if he falls and hurts himself while he's playing? That could make me look like the worst parent to the other parents!"

Using the word "or" might sound like, "Yes, he could fall, but it's highly likely that it would just be a minor hurt and he'll have learned a valuable lesson that he wouldn't be able to learn any other way."

As you can see, the power of "or" turns the parent away from being laser-focused on the child's every move, and creating anxiety, to accepting the outcome, and trusting that some good may come from the fall should the child fall.

Here's another example:

A man walks into a shopping mall and feels overwhelmed by the number of people there. A thought shows up that says, "You better be careful; you may need to call the ambulance in case you have a panic attack, which would possibly make you look weak and fragile to your community."

Or, the man could think to himself, "This feeling is just an initial reaction to a different environment, and it will pass just like it always has."

I want to emphasize something very important to make sure each and every one of these and the other responding skillsets are used most effectively: You must act in line with your response! If you use The Power of Or, and create boredom and disinterest over the catastrophic idea only to go sit in the food court with your hoodie on after just walking into the mall, you're doing nothing to convince your inner child of safety. Instead, if you go into your favorite retail store and begin feeling the material of the clothing and sparking a conversation with the store clerk, you've done a great job of defying the irrational fear. Is this easy? Most definitely not; it's meant to create small daily wins that will pull you out of anxiety and into inner freedom. So make sure to again build on the new response mentally, and act in line with the new response you've just executed, no matter what you feel you want to do.

Here are a few more examples of taking empowered action while allowing your limiting thoughts and feelings to subside:

- Walk around your house backward
- Call a friend and talk about your progress
- Try on a pair of new shoes in a store
- Take a cold shower

- Read
- Take a walk around the block

These are all examples of behaviors that follow all three categories of responding. You can come up with your own list of many more. And as long as they oppose what you'd normally do in those situations, that's good enough.

Physiological Responding

The goal of physiological responding is to show you powerful ways of working with your body to create an instant change in your emotional state. The biggest part of your subconscious mind is your body, so if we can get the body involved in empowering ways, it will help with our perceptions and actions as well (heck, it'll even help with how you perceive memories). Every emotional state has a corresponding way we stand and how we breathe. Depressed people look helpless and breathe shallowly, so do anxious people. People who live in inner peace, however, look and breathe differently, hence feeling differently. Through the works of social psychologist Amy Cuddy we now understand that when we hold what she refers to as "Power Poses" for 2 minutes, we relax 20-40% more, as well as experience a rise in testosterone. This is tried and tested. If you'd like to learn more about power poses, check out Amy's excellent TED talk on YouTube.

Speed

In physiological responding, our first focus will be on speed. The speed in which you do things throughout the day communicates with your nervous system, telling it what is threatening to your survival, and what is safe.

Slowing down makes you more present, which gives the conscious mind the ability to question the negatives, and to be able to change a person's perceptions. As we become more aware of our speed, we become more engaged in our five senses. We begin to actually taste our food instead of rushing through it to get to the next thing to do, we begin to hear the sounds of nature rather than the irrational fears within our minds, and we begin to see the miracles around us that we would normally miss. I've worked with many people in the past who've been able to overcome their anxieties just by consciously slowing down as they go about their day.

Here are the three main rules you must be aware of with speed:

1) Prepare yourself to begin slowing down more. This means waking up a few minutes earlier to get to work on time.

2) Shoot for engaging in a speed that is 50-70% of what your normal is. If you usually eat a meal in 3 minutes, take 6 minutes. If you normally drive at 60 mph, drive at 45 mph. You get the idea.

3) Bring into your awareness the three things you do the fastest. For me, it was eating, talking, and walking. I began focusing on staying within the 50-70% speed range for all three of these and, in turn, found myself getting less anxious.

The first few days of reducing your speed will feel uncomfortable; I can promise you that. But aren't we here to welcome discomfort since we know it's the very path toward healing? Absolutely. One more thing to note with speed that will be helpful is to bring a reminder with you throughout the day. Write the letter S (for speed) on the back of your hand or wear a ring if you like. As soon as you become aware of the letter S or the object, you'll turn your attention right back to moving at the right speed.

Breathing

Many people have heard about the importance of proper breathing as a tool for healing anxiety, but they don't really know any practical skills. Just telling someone to slow down their breathing isn't enough; again, we're dealing with specific needs here. How slow is slow? Is it nose in, mouth out, or the other way around? And for how long? The more specific, the more focused you'll become on your breathing in a way that helps you rather than hurts your progress.

Behind the simple act of breathing lies a process that affects us all profoundly. It affects the way we think and feel; it affects the quality of what we create and how we function in our daily lives. Hyperventilation not only causes more anxiety, but it also can aggravate a variety of bodily symptoms that may make someone think that they are developing a physical disease. When the anxiety sufferer spots the abnormal breathing pattern and successfully trains themselves to shift from maladaptive (coping) to rhythmic breathing patterns, they will feel it in a positive way. Hyperventilation (or over-breathing) means that you expel carbon dioxide (CO_2) faster than your body is producing it. This usually occurs with rapid and shallow "chest breathing."

Why is shallow breathing a problem?

This is a problem because when blood CO_2 drops, at least two major changes occur in the body:

1) The acidity in the blood changes, causing less oxygen to reach the tissues.
2) Blood vessels constrict, causing the brain to receive less oxygen.

Shallow breathing can cause:

- Dizziness
- Numbness
- Air hunger (gasping for air)
- Excessive sighing
- Constant belching
- Excessive yawning
- Twitching
- And more

The changes in acidity in the blood play a major role in our sensitized nerves, so we must begin accompanying our new speed with a set of breathing skillsets to restore homeostasis in the body.

Square breathing

Square breathing is one of my favorite ways of responding to anxiousness via the breath. At the beginning of the practice, the square will be small, and over time we will up the time we take to go around the square. Here are the correct steps to square breathing at the beginning stage:

1) Breathe in for 4 seconds
2) Hold the breath for 4 seconds

3) Breathe out for 6 seconds
4) Hold the out-breath for 4 seconds

That's it. It's literally taking your breath all around the square. In general, nasal breathing is healthier than mouth breathing because of the greater air pressure and natural slowness in the exhalation, providing the lungs with extra time to release a larger amount of oxygen. Keep this in mind for all of these breathing skillsets. Square breathing can be used to counter shallow breathing, unhelpful thoughts, or physical sensations in your body. Do your best to be in the moment with the breath, rather than focusing on whether it's working or not; this is essential for all these tools.

Rhythmic abdominal breathing

Our goal is to turn from erratic breathing rhythms to slow, rhythmic breathing. Some people master breath responding quickly, while others can take months to automate the new patterns. Either way, it doesn't matter; keep practicing as much as you can throughout the day, as there's no limit to the amount of breathwork you can implement.

Here are the steps for rhythmic abdominal breathing:

1) Lie on your back.
2) Place a book over your abdomen. This will encourage abdominal movement and provide resistance to strengthen the diaphragm.
3) Begin a 4-second in and 8-second out breathing rhythm as we place more emphasis on a longer exhale for all our breathing responses. This is because the inhalation stimulates the

sympathetic system more (fight, flight, freeze), whereas the exhale activates the parasympathetic system more (rest and digest).

4) Keep going until you feel a steady shift in your emotional and physical state.

Rhythmic abdominal breathing requires an environment where you can lie down. This is compared to square breathing, which can be practiced anywhere, anytime. Remember, as much as these three breathing exercises are catered to countering unhelpful breathing patterns, they can be utilized anytime. Even when you're in a neutral-to-pleasant emotional state, you can still keep practicing. When we are constantly under anxiety, we tend to tense the muscles in our chest, abdomen, throat, and neck. This creates a cycle of higher and higher states of arousal, forcing the person into seeing everyday normal inner and outer occurrences as dangerous. Through this breathing exercise, we'll begin developing a sense of lightness as we give ourselves what we truly deserve, inner peace.

Nostril breathing

If you've ever been to a yoga class, it's quite common that nostril breathing is a part of the warm-up or cooldown of the class. I love nostril breathing, even though at the start, I felt awkward. A few of my most significant findings with nostril breathing were that it enhanced my mental functioning and sharpened my mental clarity, as well as enhanced the quality of my sleep. Let's get into the steps:

1) Sit comfortably, place your right hand on your knee, and your left hand on your left nostril.

2) Inhale deeply through your right nostril, plug your right nostril with one of your fingers, exhale fully through your left nostril.
3) Inhale through your left nostril, plug your left nostril with one of your fingers, exhale fully through your right nostril.
4) This is one cycle.
5) Continue until your emotional state and your thinking change.

Nostril breathing may be more challenging if a person is already in a very heightened state of anxiety. But remember that with all of these responding practices, we are catching the negatives at the beginning, not waiting until a full-blown anxiety attack to respond. As we strengthen our awareness around these practices daily, we will meet with pleasant anticipation of irrational fear, and be prepared with our TFH (toolbox for healing). Remember, these are tools to bring about disinterest and boredom toward cognitive distortions, balance within the nervous system, and safety toward the inner wounded child. They are not to be seen as the very techniques for healing, but instead a gateway to deeper understanding that will then lead to freedom.

Auditory Responding

Anxiety is a physical response, and yet it can't be generated without a certain degree of respect for the voice we hear in our minds. Auditory responding is one of the quickest ways of turning a negative perception into a neutral one. This is done through a certain degree of imagination and distorting the way we hear the negative thoughts within us. Auditory responding gets us back in touch with a necessary part within us that we've lost along the way — playfulness. Through this response, we can re-engage with our creativity and find the ridiculousness in our limited ways of thinking, and begin ridiculing these ideas within.

Change the tone

Who do the voices in your head sound like? How close or far away are they? Is it more of a low or higher pitch? Imagining altering the way we listen to these voices, how would that make a difference in our reactions to them? The answer is, it would make a tremendous difference. This auditory response alone has the power to leave catastrophic thinking in the dust. It has that potential because of all the neural connections we've already made in our brains: this means that; that means this; he's funny; she's too serious; life is …; etc.

These connections form our reality. So what if we could use less threatening pairings and input them within the voices of fear that are currently leading to anxiety? Here are the steps to begin changing the tone:

1) Close your eyes and think about a funny cartoon character you enjoyed when you were a child. This could be anyone from Bugs Bunny, to Goofy, to the Tasmanian Devil (although he's also in need of some anxiety coaching, so pick someone else).

2) As you choose your cartoon character, come face to face with them in your mind's eye. As you imagine being face to face with your funny cartoon character, begin listening to one of those

negative, intrusive thoughts that have been weighing heavily on you lately through the exact tone of voice of that character.

3) As you listen to that fear-based thought in the tone of that cartoon character, also notice how their lips are moving, how Bugs is chomping on his carrot, or how Goofy is so clumsy.

4) Listen to that thought AS MANY TIMES AS IT TAKES to create a neutral emotional response to it. When you feel like this thought will no longer take up your focus and affect your emotional state in a negative manner, open your eyes.

The key phrase here is "do as many repetitions as it takes." The power behind auditory responding is in its repetition. Some people may need to hear it five times, some 50 times until they're ready to see the same situation from a whole other perspective. As with all auditory responding skillsets, you'll need a few moments to yourself to implement them. This means that if you're in a crowded and hectic environment, go to the restroom for a few minutes. Since changing the tone is the only one out of the three auditory responding skills that utilizes a high degree of conscious imagination, you'll also need your eyes closed to get the most out of it. Don't be too concerned over the vividness of the pictures in your imagination; your nervous system can read you through your intentions and emotions already.

Super slow-mo

Super Slow-Mo will strengthen your patience (something we can all get better at) and put you in a much calmer state. This auditory response to a threatening thought has only one step to it, but don't let the simplicity of this or any other technique fool you. Remember, it's about learning to communicate in a language that the deepest parts of us can understand. When we can consistently speak that language, long-lasting changes appear.

Here's the Super Slow-Mo process:

Listen to a thought that's been holding you back from living a fulfilling life in super slow motion. Just like the old tape recorders where you could press slow motion and the voices came out sounding funny. For example, the thought "I'll never end my anxiety," would sound something like this:

"I'lllllllllllllllllll neeeeeeeeeeeeevvvvvvvvvvvvvvvvveeeeerrrrrrrrrrrr eeeeeeeeennnnnddddddddddddd myyyyyyyyyyyyyyyyyyyyy annnnnnnnxxxxxxxxiiiiiiiiiieeeeettttttyyyyyyyyyyyyyyyy."

That's a lot of letters, but you get the point. Again, run Super Slow-Mo as many times as you need to in order to feel differently about the thought. This way, you'll get your focus turned from being in your head (internal) to engaged again in your outside world (external).

Listen at a distance

Having fun yet? This one's legendary; just ask many of my clients who've gone through my programs. Listening At A Distance is a one-step process as well and can be used for any situation where you begin thinking the worst. Take a few moments now to think about a recent event when someone was telling you something from a distance, and how you felt about it, compared to someone telling you the same thing while standing right next to you. The first one holds very little interest to you while you have no choice but to be fully engaged with the second one.

Here's the step:

Listen to a negative thought that you've been giving way too much attention to lately as if you hear it from 100 feet away. Don't be too concerned about the tone; just notice that it's more like a whisper now rather than a shout, as it has been lately.

You may find that your body begins moving toward the place where that voice is coming from out of habit. It's hard to hear, so you adjust yourself to get a better grasp; this is natural. When listening at a distance you may feel like you're in quite an unfamiliar place since the voice in your head has been so close and loud for so long. This is normal; it's the process toward healing. Embrace that moment, find freedom in distancing yourself from these words, and see how quickly you can shift your focus onto one of the miracles in your life.

Practice each of these three auditory responses now before moving on to the next chapter. Which one brought you to disinterest and boredom the fastest, and which one brought you to a neutral emotional state the quickest? You want to master all three of them, of course, but if there's one that speaks to you more powerfully than the others, start responding with that one.

Now your TFH (toolbox for healing) is filled with the only skillsets you'll need to bring yourself from internally sensitized to externally aware. Enjoy the progress; you deserve it.

Summary:

- All three of these responding skillsets can be used at any given moment. Get your feet wet and begin practicing them as you check your emotional state and recognize which ones speak the most powerfully to you.

- Approach each of these with the intention that your negative thoughts and physical feelings will be subsiding gradually. The last thing you want is to bring your TFH with you throughout the day, implement them, and have your emotional state begin shifting but not at the rate and speed that you want. In turn, you will label the skillset as not working. It's never the skills; it's a component within the person that holds back the skill from fully working. Remember this; it's a crucial lesson.

- The goal is automation. To make these new skillsets automatic over time so you don't have to use your conscious mind to go through the steps. You just unconsciously do it when the opportunity presents itself.

- In the first week, responding will feel very much like work. Accept this; it's different, it goes against your norm, and it's what you need.

- Gradually turn from needing someone around you during sensitizing moments to knowing you've got the tools to handle any situation on your own, which is a powerful transition.

CHAPTER 21:

Preventing Anxiety In Kids: For Parents Or Caregivers

"Study yourself much more than you study others."

As a child, I experienced tremendous worry from moment to moment. I often tell people that I had a clinically diagnosed anxiety disorder for 6 years, yet I suffered from anxiety for 25 years. I'm sure now, looking back, that my grandfather, father, tennis coaches, and even a few of my teachers didn't take into account how I would perceive what had been playing out. In their eyes, it seemed I would go through a difficult experience with them, eventually we would talk it out or hug it out, and it would be done. Little did they realize that anyone I deemed as an authority — a developmental figure — was like a loaded weapon walking around me. Their words stung deeper than 100 wasps; their constant neglect made me wonder what I had done wrong, and their physical abuse tore away pieces of my soul. I felt like I was always on edge, even though on the outside, I had begun mastering my persona of "everything is fine." On the inside, however, there was a bewildered little boy looking for the pieces of the puzzle that would start connecting in order to please the authority figures. Conscious parenting existed through the nurturing, broad perspectives of my mother, whereas my father's bar was set too high to be met.

A child growing up in any generation can me bet with tremendous difficulty should conscious parenting not be fulfilled. If a parent neglects their own inner work, there's no chance they can provide their child with the balance and guidance they need. But if a parent doesn't believe there's a problem going on with them that needs to be solved, no action will be taken.

1-in-8 kids today worldwide suffer from an anxiety disorder. Children are being put on antidepressants at staggering rates because their inner distress isn't understood at the level it needs to be. We blame the child more than we blame the environments and the people in them. This needs to end as we begin peeling back the layers behind the formula that kids use in their minds and bodies that create their inner distress.

No child is a hopeless case, but many sure feel that way. Kids need to be kids, but that can be hard to do if every mistake they make comes with a verbal and emotional beating. Some parents take advantage of the lack of conscious resources a child has. They place strain and blame over the child simply to release their own inner rage as the opportunity presents itself in the moment. This kind of discharge can make the parent feel a little better temporarily. Still, they will run into a similar scenario soon again due to not dealing with the roots of their own emotional repression.

Having brought this into the open, though, let's also take into consideration that the parent is doing what he or she believes is best for the child. No parent wants to see their child become a sensitized worrywart (although, unconsciously, a big part of the parent would prefer the child become just like them out of sheer survival instinct). This goes on below the level of conscious awareness; it's energetic. This becomes apparent between the first 9 months a child is in the womb. As the mother's emotional state changes from moment to moment, the child picks up on these changes. The thoughts, words, intentions, imagery, and actions all affect the child within the womb. This period of time becomes a very important part of the child's overall development.

In order to prevent, lessen, and eventually help end a child's anxious ways, let's look at three of what I believe are the most important steps a parent must take:

Replace the words 'be careful' with 'be aware'

You hear it far too often; the loving intentions by mom and dad expressed through the words, "be careful." Be careful literally means "be afraid!" To carefully do something translates into "tiptoeing" around what you are about to do since danger could lurk at any moment. The more the child hears the words "be careful," the more they believe that life might take a turn for the worst at any moment. Caregivers must commit to a vocabulary that strengthens the thinking mind, not the survival and emotional minds of a child (therefore, this level of consciousness will affect the

265

parent positively as well). To begin this process, replace the words "be careful" with "be aware."

"Be aware" expresses a calm recognition over the situation without activating the stress response. "Be aware" doesn't express the need to look for danger in the situation; instead, it allows the person to be more involved in the situation. This new term holds much more power than you'd think since almost every word a child hears after the age of 5 already has an association connected to it.

Kids trance out much faster during everyday situations than adults do because of their developing conscious minds. When someone gives a talk, for example, depending on the word expressed, people begin zoning out and mentally going elsewhere. They will zone out depending on whether the words the speaker expressed come with a highly emotional experience from the listener's past. This means that during the development of the child's mind, we must be aware of what terms we're consistently using.

Small shifts in the words being expressed can lead to big changes in the child's emotional state. If this shift becomes consistent, their level of arousal will lessen as the child begins sorting for more good in their world rather than what could go wrong. Caregivers can certainly get quite experimental with this as well, trying out different words and recognizing how the child responds to them based on their physiology.

A person's body will tell you everything you need to know about what they're thinking, feeling, and imagining. Kids give it away much easier than adults do. So, if you see an empowered child who looks pleased in the moment, you know the words you expressed prior and during that situation are working well. If, however, the child seems hesitant and is getting flustered quickly, they may be unconsciously sorting for danger and becoming angry more quickly. Remember, awareness is good; carefully acting is not. What's repeated becomes habit and habit becomes a part of the personality of the child as they move on with their lives. We want to build empowering habits, not disempowering ones. We don't want the child thinking the world is scarier than what it really is, since what a person believes at a core level becomes their reality. You may take this valuable information and explain to the child the importance of this kind of inner dialogue, as well. They must realize that they have an option to think however they choose to in order to make the future event a pleasant experience. Teach them that they don't have to believe everything they feel. That knowledge will empower them.

Reframing recent experiences together

Within the RIC framework, reframing can also be utilized by kids. They do it every day all day anyway! Let's just start teaching them how to do it consciously rather than succumb to unconsciously reliving the past over and over in negative ways. Reframing the past for the child can easily turn into a 5-minute after-school habit as long as they understand the wonders and magic of it all. I remember my grandmother back when I was around 7 years old, telling me that my imagination held the key to my eternal happiness. She was a smart woman, as you can already tell, since she understood the elements that make a child so carefree and embracing future uncertainty.

Reframing for kids happens when you either sense or hear a child express a recently unpleasant event. It could have been anything, from being ridiculed at school to answering a teacher's question incorrectly, to failing a test, etc. Instead of the child suppressing the experience in their long-term memory, it's important to reframe it in the emotional language that the subconscious will understand. This way, the child begins to perceive the event from different angles and begins feeling differently about the whole thing. This creates a beautiful snowball effect in a positive direction, as they don't feel as sensitive to a similar experience they may face in the future. As the subconscious mind and body check into the infinite memory system, it looks for what took place first and last connected to the present situation. So, when the reframing process takes place, that process will lead to a much more emotionally neutral child, which is just what we want. The steps are easy since the child already possesses a vivid imagination:

Step 1) Hold hands with the child, close your eyes, and relax as best you both can (don't shoot for perfection).

Step 2) Tell the child to imagine the event happening again in their mind's eye, but in a way where it's a much more pleasant experience. If they could redo the whole thing, and have a pleasant experience, how would they want it to go? Allow them to go through the beginning, middle, and end of the experience, reframing it as they go. Make sure they know that they're allowed to get emotionally invested in their experience.

Step 3) Allow them to open up their eyes when the experience has been reframed and share with you the main lesson they learned. Things such as, "I realize that I made it bigger than what it really was," or "I could have reacted totally differently" usually come up. Tell them to write down their lesson in their reframing journal. Follow the above process whenever the need to reframe an unpleasant situation arises.

Holding hands with your child through the process emphasizes safety. The message is: It's safe to see the experience differently through your mind's eye so you can see the experience differently in the physical world. As the child's emotional state shifts about the experience, so will their physical experience as time goes on. Once the child is in a more pleasant emotional state over the event, so will the flow of the event shift should it show up again in the future.

Since we're always in communication with everything and everyone, our subconscious mind makes evaluations over everything far before the conscious mind does. The challenge with reframing for children is to be able to keep their focus on one thing for an extended time. This is where patience is key. Even a 1-minute process can completely alter the child's perceptions over the event. So don't shoot for an extended time, communicate the importance of emotional absorption for the child during reframing instead. Eventually, they'll become more and more engaged and focused, which will translate into responding to physical situations in a more controlled manner.

Allowing more mistakes

A child who isn't allowed to make mistakes never learns how to think for themselves. Also, as the child grows up, they may have the mistaken belief that as long as they follow the rules of life, nothing can go wrong. All of a sudden, a problem arises, and they have no idea what to do. This can lead the child into tremendous anxiety, which then can lead to avoidance behaviors and catastrophic thinking. When authority figures present an environment to the child that has a healthy cycle of making mistakes, learning from them, and applying those lessons next time, we're creating true warriors.

Children should respect their authority figures, not worship them

By worshipping them, they stay enslaved to their rules of life and create a mental connection to their beliefs, which can be hard to break free from later down the road. As parental observing overtakes rigidness, we succeed in putting power back into the child's mind. Here are a few examples of allowing more mistakes:

- While skating with the child, intentionally fall, and once you have, laugh and make a joke out of it.
- While coloring with the child, color outside the lines.
- While telling your child a bedtime story, allow the main character to be kind of goofy and fun-loving while turning the whole story into an experience that promotes flexibility over seriousness.

As a parent, find the opportunities when you'd typically be displeased and react with anger, and turn your response to the situation around 180 degrees. Not only will this new response emphasize a more open outlook to mistakes for the child, but it will also make a lasting impression on you. Your anxiety will lessen, and people will begin noticing these changes within you. Many times, in the relationships between caregiver and child, we become obsessed with controlling every word, action, and even thought of the child because of our personal addiction to control. We feel it's the right thing to do as a parent until we take a step back and evaluate. We then begin seeing what direction the child is going … straight toward an anxiety disorder should your strict lessons be taken to heart enough times. This is all under our control. We can control the words we use, the way we imaginatively help to reprocess a child's unpleasant experience, and promote flexibility in their actions by making more mistakes. These three approaches make up the spine of what you must begin working on with your child.

Children don't need drugs as much as they need the tools to deal with their everyday challenges. They need to be taught things that we, as parents, weren't taught when we were young. As the weeks and months go by, the parent will find that the child becomes much easier to communicate with and understand. They're no longer frantic in the emotional sense but clear in the verbal sense. Their words begin to promote further progress and their perceptions begin turning toward optimism for the future. At this point, you can be proud of yourself as a parent. You've defied your unhelpful parental tactics and adopted ones that create harmony between everyone. Well done!

Summary:

- Take a child's words literally when they explain their distress. Instead of just telling them what to do, show them how to do it through your actions and reframing processes. In time, the child may or may not want to partake in imaginative reframing exercises, and instead, in a moment's notice, be able to cognitively see everything differently.

- There must be a feeling of less guilt, blame, and unforgiveness within the child, and more self-love. Also, less pressure to think, speak and be a certain way. The more self-love that shows up, the less chance irrational fear will enter the mind and body of the child.

- Healing can come quickly for the child since their brains are still in a state of development. The neural connections can be reorganized and their emotional states can shift.

- Use these three approaches with your child and it will, in turn, affect you as the parent positively as well, so commit to the process.

- As a parent, keep asking yourself the question, "What's fun about this?" while with your child. This will help to turn your focus quickly from potential risks and irrational threats to the experience that needs your full, loving support. "What's fun about this" will get you building on things you may miss should your focus strictly be turned toward fear.

CHAPTER 22:

Dealing With Setbacks

"Don't trust everything you feel. Many times your mind has no idea of the reality of the situation."

It's never failure, always feedback, and feedback is the breakfast of warriors. On the journey toward healing anxiety, we will run into setbacks, sometimes many times over. A setback is when a person has been gaining a certain amount of momentum in terms of thinking, feeling, acting, and imagining things differently, and all of a sudden, one of those four aspects comes to a halt. Either something in the external world happens, or the person is reminded of something in their mind, and the wheels begin quickly turning in the opposite direction. Suddenly, the person who was making such great progress over anxiety begins questioning themselves as they get caught up fully in the setback.

Not anticipating setbacks, and blowing them out of proportion, are two weaknesses many people have today during the anxiety-healing process. I know I did for quite some time. The moment I started thinking the worst after a week of pleasant thoughts and feelings, I beat myself up, sometimes literally. The idea of going back into severe anxiety is so frightening that when we attach ourselves to the possibility of this happening, we're already creating a snowball effect that takes us backward.

A setback is nothing more than a message. It's trying to tell you something, and we need to listen to that message loud and clear. The message could be that you simply need to hydrate more, eat more consciously, get more rest, release more repressed anger over that incident 12 years ago, connect with people, or anything else.

The acronym for some of the biggest reasons for anxiety setbacks comes down to:

H) Hunger
A) Anger
L) Loneliness
T) Tiredness

All four of these are quite self-explanatory. Hunger refers to what you're eating and how often you're eating as low blood sugar levels can affect your emotional state. Anger refers to what's still being held onto from past situations. Loneliness comes down to whether you feel fulfilled within your current social circles. Tiredness is taking on too much too often, and many times too fast, after the sense of feeling better. If all four of these are off, watch out! The conscious mind no longer has a say in what's going on and the person turns into a saber-toothed tiger wandering the streets looking for it's next victim to drop some emotional baggage on.

It's important to slow down, take a deep breath, and recognize how you got into this cycle again. As we begin understanding the message that setbacks offer, we can begin to become better inner problem solvers. The last thing you want to do in this frantic state is to believe the first two or three things your mind tells you. Because most of the time, the fourth or fifth thoughts are much more factual. The first initial ideas speak through the survival and emotional brain, as the analytical mind slowly begins to show up through patience and self-compassion.

You're not where you think you are ... yet

Since it takes 21 days to begin shifting old beliefs into new ones, we must understand that we're in the transition. We haven't gotten to the point of unconscious competence where our inner peace becomes as automatic as our anxiety once was. Unconscious competence is automatically being able to see the good in things no matter what, and it's also a place where fear is kept in its rightful place when it's actually needed. Just prior to the setback, people will think they can take on more hours at work, speak to more and more people, eat junk food, watch stimulating movies again, and so forth. Think about the inner child within you, and notice how overwhelmed he or she might be by you introducing all of these new activities to them. The most challenging thing that anyone will ever have to do is to change who they are. That's the idea behind this whole process; not so much just healing anxiety by itself. There are a few things you can and can't do in this context:

You Can:

- Challenge yourself daily by exposing yourself gradually to new experiences.

- Love yourself more for taking on a journey many would never attempt.
- - Ask for valuable advice on maintaining progress from other anxiety success stories.

You Can't:

- Flip everything around and believe you won't hit a setback by taking on way too much, too early.
- Stop applying the habits that got you into the healing transition.
- Start doing things that you know are harmful toward your emotional health, thinking that you can handle it now and that you've grown a thicker skin.

A setback means that just for a brief moment (hopefully), you've allowed your unconscious imagination to overtake your conscious one. Your conscious imagination generates pictures in your head of future events going the right way, as your protective unconscious imagination looks to show you the worst possible scenario in the hopes that you don't do what you set out to do. That inner child is feisty; I can say that. He or she doesn't give up their perspectives easily (although change can and does happen quickly as well for many who apply the teachings within RIC).

During setbacks, many people get too caught up in the outcome, when the process should take center stage in their heads instead. Enjoy the process of personal expansion and growth. I got to a point where I neither got too caught up emotionally in my small wins nor did I get too caught up in my setbacks; I just kept going. This attitude takes you to a less judgmental place, therefore creating less chance for more setbacks in the future. Even if something doesn't go the way you'd like, you find yourself brushing it off, and within 15 seconds, it's not important enough to think about anymore. This is the real you; the you that understands yourself and life better, knowing that setbacks come with the exact messages we need to hear.

Since we now know that setbacks are disguised as challenges, we can set ourselves up for a beautiful comeback. The greatest of setbacks come during times of significant positive momentum, and discouragement is not an option. An inner refusal to get caught up in these setbacks is one of the vital characteristics that bring people fully out of anxiety. It's a certain level of stubbornness that creates the flow that takes a person back into positive progress. Everyone has this stubbornness within them. I mean you have or had anxiety, didn't you? Didn't you consciously and unconsciously find ways to keep it around? The constant fear of fully letting go and embracing change and uncertainty. Yes, this stubbornness is within and now you must use it in a better way. To move through setbacks swiftly is to inspire others, and to inspire others is to meet your true purpose in this world.

We fear what we are capable of more than anything else, and you have a voice that needs to become louder over time. This voice can't be strengthened unless your mindset is right when it comes to setbacks; you expect them, and you prepare your Toolkit For Healing in response to them. Become aware that you aren't just plowing through your setback, because you may miss the lesson it brings and make the same mistakes again.

This idea of fighting past a setback will harm you more than it will help you. This is because you will become stuck on distraction methods over analytical ones. Distracting yourself only buys you more time before the inevitable downfall happens again. Over and over, you find yourself fighting through a setback, never having realized that the ultimate answer could be a simple tweak you have to make.

As you can see now, there's a time to get emotional, and there's a time to think. One must not outweigh the other, or suffering will take place again. This past addiction is not where we're going; you don't live there anymore, but you are grateful for those past experiences and what they taught you.

Physical illness setbacks

A pre-warning about what I'm about to share with you. The mind-body connection can't be neglected, and because this is the case, I must open your eyes to the realities of developing physical ailments. This is so that we can create deep insight and understanding within you rather than frighten you (should you suffer from severe health anxiety, for example). With that said, let's understand the process of developing a physical ailment, and working with this type of setback.

When a person experiences intense emotion, these emotions can become lodged in different parts of the body like energy balls. These lodged energy balls create disturbances in the body's own energy system. These energy blockages have the potential to result in physical dysfunction should stress continue to add up and accumulate within. The American Medical Association states that 60-80% of all primary-care physician visits are related to stress, and the Centers For Disease Control And Prevention believes 85% of disease is caused by some type of emotional component. Our physical bodies can be changed through the emotions we experience, so what we must start doing is focusing on this shift in emotional states. Now, let me make sure we're clear here ...

The healthiest people in the world are the ones who allow themselves to feel their emotions fully and express them fully

Fear, anger, grief, etc., are not the problems, and it's not bad to feel these. The problem is when these negative emotions don't have the opportunity to be properly released. This is where I run into a problem with today's healing methods, especially in North America, in that the methods all tackle one separate part of a much bigger picture. You'll see energy healers focusing on balancing out the energy systems in the body, without affecting change at a mental or emotional level long term. You'll see psychologists focusing on mental and behavioral shifts, without involving energetic and somatic changes (a somatic address is locating where in the body the negative emotion lives). You see my point; they are all separated, and this is why people only feel change happen temporarily for the most part.

This is where RIC teachings differ because it takes all the necessary components into consideration. Responding practices will affect mental and behavioral change, and reframing (visualization) and somatic reframing (body-centered visualization) processes affect change at an emotional and energetic level. So now that we understand how you may have developed a physical disturbance in the body, let me share a remarkable, true story with you:

My mother, who had recently turned 63, was diagnosed with ovarian cancer by three different doctors. Not only this but when the imaging scans came back, they showed a tumor in her stomach as well. Now let me ask you something, do you have an emotional parent? Times your parent's emotional intensity level by five, and you'll get my mother; she is a firecracker with no filter. Within a year of being diagnosed, her brother and father had passed away, and the timing of her cancer fits in with the time my grandpa had just passed perfectly. She told me how she fell to the ground in utter shock after hearing this diagnosis since the C-word meant the end for her. When she came to, she called me as I was finishing up a seminar just outside of Vancouver, BC. I was also in shock, but once that shock subsided, I felt a sense of peace come over me. I tried to fight it away, thinking it wasn't the right way to react at that moment since this was all new to me, but I quickly realized that inner balance was the key to thinking straight.

A few weeks went by and with it came some miraculous changes. The combination of alkalizing her body, and a diet overhaul (that included juicing with additions like turmeric, black seed oil, ginger, and other herbs) were implemented. Her mindset began to change and she was much more present in the now. Couple these nutritional changes with powerful somatic reframing processes with me where we allowed her to speak to her father and brother to create closure was key. She cried like never before; she had forgiven herself since she carried plenty of guilt for not feeling like she had done enough for them, as well she got forgiveness from them. She listened to my YouTube affirmations nightly playing in the background before dozing off to sleep. These changes weren't just at a mental level, but a physiological one; her body began responding positively. She also began implementing grounding on grassy fields barefoot as she began feeling an even deeper connection with the earth.

As the surgery date neared, the doctors told us both that they would be preparing her body with the insertion of a tube for chemotherapy. Me and mom both refused this, as we had other ideas. The surgery went extremely well, and what the surgeon removed was a benign cyst, to the joy of her and everyone involved.

This was a true miracle, and we believed that miracles happen on a daily basis, so why not to Mom. She began believing in the creative intelligence that lived within her. If she could just come into contact with this intelligence somehow, she felt she could reverse what she was told she had. She realized the connection in how her emotions and attitude had changed within the year due to the passing of my grandfather and uncle, and she began transitioning toward a whole new outlook on herself and life.

My mom suffered a physical setback, as many people right now might be going through, and she recognized the importance of reinventing who she was and getting to the root of her physical issue. No one could convince her of this necessary shift; only she could do it, and I'm proud to say she owned it 100%. This capability is present in each and every one of us, and you must believe me that it is.

I've visited "alternative" treatment centers around Asia, and shamanistic practices, and have witnessed incredible changes in the emotional, physical, and spiritual bodies of people. In fact, scientist Gregg Braden has a fascinating story about visiting a drug-free hospital in China. As he shares the story, three doctors surround a patient living with a tumor in her stomach. The words, "the healing is here," and "it is done," begin getting louder and more emotional moment to moment until just a few minutes into the process, you can visibly see the tumor of this woman shrink and disappear on the scanner. A miraculous moment that was caused by the collective mental environments of everyone involved, as well as the emotional energy that communicated with the inner intelligence of the patient until the healing showed up. These stories should get you excited about the healing potentials we all have access to within us. Having brought this inner potential to your awareness, however, you must follow your doctor's orders whenever possible while doing the inner work simultaneously.

The words I'll never forget from my mother after all this were, "That was some wake-up call." A wake-up call that filled her with such tremendous gratitude for life that anyone who was near her felt it. If you're currently going through a physical challenge, see it as your wake-up call as well. Once overcome, you'll never look at life quite the same way again, and you'll fully realize the power you have within you.

Summary:

- You are only limited by what you believe.
- Setbacks are learning opportunities to recognize the structure that led to the setback.
- Setbacks can be used positively or be seen as going backward; the choice is always yours.
- One of the most vital characteristics of people who've transformed their identity and overcome anxiety is their ability to move past setbacks swiftly.
- Use setbacks as an opportunity to show your inner child an opposing viewpoint over what took place next time you're in the same situation.

The Key Ingredient – Trust

*"Work toward becoming who you
needed when you were young."*

Trust is something that many people who embark on positive change work find extremely challenging. When referring to trust, I'm first speaking about trusting in yourself. Put aside all the past disappointments you've encountered while working toward ending your anxiety. That was then; this is now. The two questions I have for you that I'd like you to ponder are:

Why will this time be different?

What have you learned from your past efforts that weren't fruitful in the end?

These are important questions because, as Albert Einstein said, "The definition of insanity is doing the same thing over and over again, and expecting different results." In this context, that same thing that he's referring to could come down to the same attitudes, perceptions, actions, or otherwise. This time must be different in every which way. What will be the most different part of this journey is that you will trust in your inner wisdom and capabilities to turn this around. With more and more small wins that you encounter, the more inner trust will be built, and the more trust that you begin building in yourself to make this change happen, the faster everything around you starts to change. Not so much physically, but perceptually. Trust in the day as you wake up, knowing you've already won by living one more day on this beautiful planet. Trust in a higher power that you allow in to become the co-creator of the new you. This co-creator or source energy has only the best intentions for you. It wants you to excel in every which way so that you can give back to others in time.

One of the biggest reasons I lacked trust in myself was because I didn't like change. What anxiety sufferer really does? If we don't utilize our conscious minds and see through the negative labels we've placed toward change, it won't get any easier. In fact, it will just get harder. So you must agree to change and love change. You must welcome in fear rather than avoid it. Winston Churchill said, "If you're going through hell, keep going." What that means in the anxiety world is to see through irrational fear, and act on it. But again, I could write 10 books telling you all the things you must do; in the end, it comes down to whether you're ready to make time for you, and understand that your current formula for change isn't working.

These two aspects can be challenging since we live in a world that is nonstop and expects more and more from us every day. I was in that world for years until I realized that I could work toward a new way of living in the world. I had worked 60 hours a week, slaving away as an assistant tennis coach for $13.75 an hour, and that was after six years of being in the same tennis club! During those days, I got to know suffering very well, and I also mastered my artificial smile to the point where people asked me why I was so positive all the time. If they only knew about the volcano within me that was ready to explode at any moment.

I kept telling myself, "If I could imagine it, I could create it." So I began imagining what I wanted during the two times of the day I could directly influence my subconscious mind: the first 15 minutes of the day, and the last 15 minutes of the day. I engaged in a process called "image cycling" that the great Bill Bengston coined around "The Bengston Method," where I took the seven to 10 most important aspects of my life and I asked myself ...

If these aspects of my life were just the way I wanted them to be, what would that look like, sound like, and feel like?

Notice the sensory-based language. At first, I focused on my health. I would see myself in my mind's eye getting checked by the doctor and the doctor being shocked at how I had become so healthy, followed by walking out of his office with a blue healing aura that oozed good health. In this aspect, I also pictured others pointing at me saying, "Is that Dennis? The healthiest man in the world? I wish I could be more like him." After a 10-second run of that ideal movie in my mind, I moved on to relationships, where I saw a few new like-minded people come into my life, and together, we were all having a pleasant conversation. We would joke, argue, smile, and drink tea. I loved it.

After running my 10-second movie on relationships, I would move on to contribution, travel, leisure time, family, and more. I would cycle through these two or three times in a row in the morning and at night. I began trusting. I began getting more and more hopeful, and more and more engaged in what was happening around me. I was becoming less concerned about potential failures, perfectionism, and pleasing others, and more focused on enjoying the feelings of future freedom.

Image cycling showed me what was possible in a world I trusted very little at the time. I found myself getting more and more dissatisfied with living a life where I would barely see my family and slaving to a boss I hated. Most people never grow out of what they hear from others about life. They are slaves to their parents who, with good intentions, teach the rules of life, followed by slaving away at school from 8 a.m. to 3 p.m. daily followed by potential detention if you said a naughty word, as well as three hours of homework. Another couple years of university (if we're really good boys and girls) where we shoot for an occupation that we believe will fulfill us, only to question if it really will just before graduating.

We move into our career with the hope that it will be all it was amped up to be only to realize our true purpose lives elsewhere. We get married and raise a family because people who stay single are seen as psychotic in the world today. We save for our retirement only to realize that the average age a person lives is only a few years past when we're eligible, and as we lie on our deathbed, we realize the opportunity we missed out on: our life!

I know I've painted a depressing picture, but until someone hits rock bottom, they'll never commit to any kind of change. So if you're there, it's time to do this in ways that most people wouldn't — to think differently and to be different. This is where the magic of living exists.

I'm telling you all this because I want you to win in this game called life, not to temporarily motivate you since that motivation won't last. The biggest reason people don't take bigger leaps toward what's possible for their lives is they check in with the statistics first. They realize how different it may seem to others and how others would think it crazy to go a separate direction, so they throw the idea aside. When I told my friends and family that one day I would live in Bali, Indonesia, place my child in a school that taught street smarts, book smarts, meditation, gardening, yoga, and such, they thought I was nuts. Top that off with sharing how my tennis coaching would come to an end and their reply was, "What else can you really do, though?" Such small-minded people; most of them were living in a caged bubble. Safety and comfort become the goal we're told to shoot for. And since we've been so accustomed to this model, we unknowingly attach ourselves to the familiar world of worry and anxiety. Until now, of course.

My dream was to live in a monastery with Tibetan monks. I found myself needing more silence, more nature, and less noise and man-made environments. I found all of that in Ubud, Bali, Indonesia, after visiting a spiritual healer they refer to as a Balian. This man pointed me toward the direction of a silent retreat, where I spent two straight months away from my family. I think people have an idea of how challenging a silent retreat is, so now times that by five and you'll get the real experience. Tea and a vegan-based diet, 3-5 hours of silent meditation daily, walks in the peaceful gardens with other visitors, it wasn't a

Tibetan monastery, but it was just what the doctor ordered. The challenging part was, of course, the beginning, as my mind came up with all the reasons it was a bad idea. This untrusting part slowly subsided though, as I went through the experience, as it always does. I learned plenty from my two months in silence. When I came back to the busy streets of Canggu, Bali, where my family and I are living at the time of writing this book, I realized how stimulating it really was, and it's still nothing compared to most parts of North America where I grew up.

In silence we find ourselves

People are afraid of silence because they believe it's not productive to spend time in silence. And meditation today is getting more and more complicated even though it's the simplicity of the practice that is the most effective. In silence, we begin to trust in a foreign voice within us; our own voice. No one can help you to build your inner trust in this voice; they can only show you it exists and that's all.

The parts of our souls that we've lost on this trauma-filled journey toward living with an anxiety disorder can be regained. Inch by inch and step by step, because slowly moving in the right direction is still progress. You must see it this way as well. As you become your greatest cheerleader, you rely on others less. Your life becomes your own creation, like a painting on a canvas, but we never realized we could be in charge of the paintbrush, the colors we use, and how big the canvas could be until now.

People look at me today as if I've achieved some kind of miracle because I overcame anxiety. I tell them it's that very part of them that can't conceive this to be possible for themselves that holds them back. Nothing is real or fake, but our thinking and feeling make it so. So let me be your friend and guiding light on this journey toward total transformation. Take a stand right here, and right now, as you promise yourself that you will never again be a victim to an idea in your head, or an opinion of another person. Those days are gone. What's to come is in your hands. Don't be one of those people who wait for just the right time and just the right feeling to do what they know is right for them. Do it now and defy your fears in the process. The most peaceful moments this earth has ever known are after the greatest storms. Go through what you need to go through within this active phase in your life to be met with inner peace and a true awakening in the end. I'll be waiting on the other side with open arms ready to welcome you into the real, free world.

Dennis